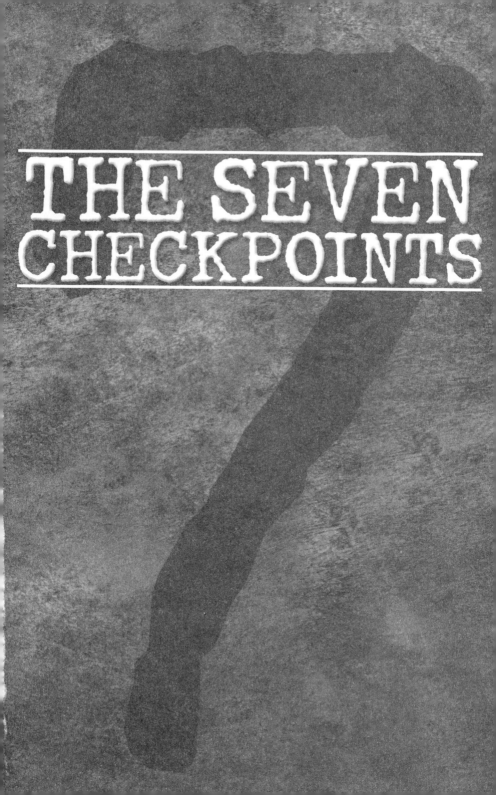

THE SEVEN
CHECKPOINTS

THE SEVEN CHECKPOINTS

Seven Principles Every Teenager Needs to Know

For Youth Leaders

ANDY STANLEY
STUART HALL

HOWARD BOOKS
A DIVISION OF SIMON & SCHUSTER
New York   London   Toronto   Sydney

Our purpose at Howard Books is to:

- *Increase faith* in the hearts of growing Christians
- *Inspire holiness* in the lives of believers
- *Instill hope* in the hearts of struggling people everywhere

Because He's coming again!

Published by Howard Books, a division of Simon & Schuster
1230 Avenue of the Americas, New York, NY 10020
www.howardpublishing.com

The Seven Checkpoints for Youth Leaders
© 2001 by Andy Stanley and Stuart Hall

Library of Congress Cataloging-in-Publication Data
Stanley, Andy.
    The seven checkpoints : seven principles every teenager needs to know : for youth leaders / Andy Stanley, Stuart Hall.
        p. cm.
    10 Digit ISBN: 1582291772; 13 Digit ISBN: 9781582291772
        1. Teenagers—Religious life. 2. Teenagers—Conduct of life. I. Hall, Stuart, 1968- II. Title.

BV 4531.2 S695 2001
259'.23—dc21

2001024271

10 9 8 7 6

HOWARD colophon is a registered trademark of Simon & Schuster, Inc.

Manufactured in the United States of America

For information regarding special discounts for bulk purchases, please contact Simon & Schuster Special Sales at 1-800-456-6798 or business@simonandschuster.com.

Edited by Michele Buckingham
Interior design by Stephanie Denney

Dedication

To the Student Ministry Team
of North Point Community Church

Contents

Contents

Foreword

Effective strategy helps us worry less about what's changing around us and focus more on what will always be true.

I began to write this foreword with the idea that student ministry is a rapidly changing, hard to grasp "thing," evolving so fast that it's almost impossible to stay on the cutting edge. But is that really true?

Let me take you back in time.

Andy Stanley and I actually met the summer before our seventh-grade year. During the height of a shaving cream free-for-all, I, being the smallest kid in the camp, took cover under a bunk bed, fearing for my life. Funny thing. Andy was already under there, his eyes as big as mine. We connected. In the heat of battle, our keen survival skills initiated a bond that has remained to this day.

Back then youth ministry was interesting. We had never heard the word *worship*; we just sang songs. The only missionary we knew of was named Lottie Moon. Lottie Moon? To have a spiritual high you had to have a really big fire and throw something in it. Sure, we counted the cost, but the idea of dying for our faith was a concept that never crossed our minds. Our biggest concern was that the Cokes and Krispy Kremes were there on Sunday morning. Life was good.

So maybe a little has changed. But a lot hasn't. We had a youth minister (they called her the youth director back then) who loved us, teachers who fed us, role models who inspired us, a pastor who poured God's Word into us, and environments that shaped us.

These days people claim the stakes are higher, but how could they be higher than they were? Every day is critical to God. The wisdom writer said, "There's nothing new under the sun." I've lived long enough to agree.

The keys to effective student ministry are the same today as they were back then. First, we need innovative leaders, those who blaze a trail with fresh creativity and not just a rehashed imitation of the current culture. Second, we must have a belief in our students' capacity to grasp more, a conviction that they can access and experience the deeper things of God. Third, we as leaders must have a genuine and living faith, empowering us to "show the way" and not just "tell the way." And fourth, we must have a clear strategy so that at the end of the day we don't just have a pile of expended energy but rather the assurance that we've accomplished the goal.

That's why what Andy Stanley and Stuart Hall have done in these pages is vital. Effective strategy helps us worry less about what's changing around us and focus more on what will always be true about us. Andy is the most strategic person I know. He's amazing to watch. He lives out what he has written down. So let him lead you and help you channel your passion and sacrifice into a pathway to progress.

One last thing (and this is for us all). Let's *live* these principles first and *teach* them second. That way we'll know at least one person in the youth group is getting it!

That's a built-in guarantee of success.

LOUIE GIGLIO

Preface

After twenty years of working with teenagers, I am convinced that there are seven basic principles every student should understand, commit to memory, and embrace before they graduate and leave the safety of their homes and youth ministries.

These seven student-specific principles are the irreducible minimum. These are the must-know, can't-be-without principles. They are not all that is important. But they are what is most important for students.

As a youth minister I've invested a great deal of time looking for useful curriculums. I've spent countless hours piecing together interesting talks. I've tried hard to find good camp speakers. I threw a lot of helpful information at my students in those early days. I'm sure some of it stuck. But how much?

Which parts? Were the things that stuck with them the things that *needed* to stick with them?

Taking Stock

After I graduated my fourth senior class, I decided it was time for some pointed evaluation. That's when I discovered I had no tool with which to evaluate. Our student ministry was growing numerically. That kept all the higher-ups happy. But I had no way of knowing how effectively I was instilling life-changing truth into the hearts of my students.

That fourth graduating class sat under my teaching from ninth through twelfth grade. But what did they learn? Did I communicate, or did I simply cover a lot of material?

At that point I gathered my staff (both of them) and began asking questions:

✔ If we could permanently imprint anything we want upon our students' minds, what would it be?

✔ What do they *need* to know? What is the irreducible minimum?

✔ When everybody else is "doing it," what's going to keep them from joining in?

✔ When they are sitting in a dorm room during their freshman year contemplating their options for the evening, what principles or truths should drift through their minds in that potentially defining moment?

This was an ongoing dialogue that lasted for several months. I would throw out one or two of these questions for discussion at every leadership meeting. Whenever I met with other youth ministers, I would ask them what they believed were the most important concepts for students to embrace. Eventually I compiled a list of twelve principles. After presenting these twelve truths to several trusted men and women in student ministry, I reduced the list to nine and eventually to seven.

Selective Memory

Let's face it. Our students will forget most of what we teach them. But hopefully they will remember *something*. We have wasted a whole lot of time preparing and teaching if they don't! And assuming they will remember something, doesn't it make sense that we determine what it is they remember?

After all, God has positioned us in the lives of our students as leaders, mentors, and friends. For a few short but strategic years, we have the opportunity and responsibility to shape their thinking. And in doing so, we have the privilege of helping set their trajectory into the future.

The Youth Ministry Dilemma

No doubt you have gained some proficiency in creating exciting and attractive environments for students. But as you know, both *context* and *content* are crucial for effective student ministry. The context—the environment—is what keeps them coming back. The content—what we communicate—is what equips students for life. If you are like me, the content side of the equation is what drew you into student ministry to begin with. You wanted to see kids' lives changed. But you quickly learned that without the right context, there wouldn't be any lives to change!

Consequently, you have been forced to spend a great deal of time and energy (and money!) creating attractive environments for students. To compound the problem, the success of your ministry is probably judged on your ability to attract students to your youth group. You don't get to hire extra staff based on the spiritual development of your students; you get staff support when the numbers demand it.

Bottom line, the context of your ministry has tended to absorb most of your attention. So, like me, you have probably come to the end of a stretch of ministry and wondered, "What did they learn?" You know what they *heard*. But what did they take away? Sure, they will remember the events and the people who were "there for them." But did they walk away with the tools and the truths they will need to survive and thrive in the world beyond high school?

The tyranny of the urgent and the quest for a larger budget are facts of youth-ministry life. You and I have got to keep creating those high-energy, pack-'em-in-tight environments. If we have a room that will seat one hundred students, we need to do everything we can to fill it up.

Once the room is full, however, let's make sure the content we throw at them sticks. Let's make it memorable. Let's make it transformational. And let's keep coming back to a handful of concepts over and over until our students dream them in their sleep. That's where the seven checkpoints come in.

Recycled Truth

This book is designed to provide you with the content for those environments you spend so much time and energy creating. My goal in writing *The Seven Checkpoints* is to give you seven principles around which you can organize the content of your entire student ministry.

I have developed two models to choose from, a two-year model and a four-year model. The idea is that in two or four years you can cycle through all seven principles several times. Each of these plans will incorporate your Sunday morning small group times, midweek services, weekend retreats, and summer camps. The seven principles have been reduced down to seven memorable phrases—phrases that you can pepper throughout your leadership training, counseling, teaching, and speaking.

Imagine meeting with the parents of your students and showing them the seven principles that serve as the foundation for all you will teach their kids.

Imagine having a content calendar that can be used to guide the development of your activity calendar throughout the year.

Imagine having a handful of carefully crafted principles to choose from in developing the theme of every camp or retreat.

These are just a few of the advantages of adopting the seven checkpoints strategy. But the greatest advantage is this: You will know that you are maximizing your input into the lives of the students God has entrusted to your care. You will know that you are changing lives. And isn't that why you got into youth ministry in the first place?

Acknowledgments

Every book represents a team effort. This one is certainly no exception. Without each of the following people, this book would never have happened.

Reggie Joiner, Kevin Ragsdale, and Heath Bennett

Your passion and vision to develop teenagers who make a difference is contagious. Thank you for championing the cause and setting the standard so high! You guys are the real heroes of this project.

Our Families

Thank you for enduring the zip disk problems, editing issues, late nights, and phone calls. We love you more than you will ever know.

Diane Grant

Thank you for being the world's greatest facilitator of information with such a heart for people. How do you do it?

Denny and Philis Boultinghouse

Thank you for believing in this project.

Michele Buckingham and Stephanie Denney

Thank you, Michele, for reading between the lines, crossing the *t*s and dotting the *i*s, and thank you, Stephanie, for the on-target book design. You guys are awesome!

What's It All About?

The Seven Checkpoints

Seven Principles Every Teenager Needs to Know

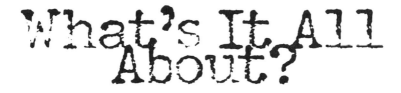

What's It All About?

The Seven Checkpoints

Seven Principles Every Teenager Needs to Know

It's a great time in history to work with teenagers!

Youth ministry has slowly evolved into a profession of professionals. What was once considered the lowest rung on the ladder in most churches has now become a job that demands respect. The fight for the souls of our teenagers has intensified. Because parents and church leaders see this, respect for the position of youth minister has increased.

We have entered the race with the likes of Hollywood and MTV for the minds and hearts of teenagers. To keep pace, youth ministries across the country have put a great deal of effort into creating the best *context* for youth ministry. We all want our ministry environments to be student-friendly. To that end we have produced camps, conferences, and weekly meetings that rival rock concerts in sight and sound.

We want to speak to teenagers in their language, and many media resources have risen to help us. The Christian music industry has grown from a slighted "phase" to a powerful influence. Our push for relevancy has produced hits in the mainstream by artists like Sixpence None the Richer, DC Talk, and P.O.D. Quality videos and television shows have been designed to help students understand who Jesus is and how to deal with the issues that are unique to their stage of life.

These new and relevant approaches to reaching the student culture are needed and refreshing. They are especially refreshing to those of us who've spent countless hours trying to convince the generation before us that an anapestic beat won't send kids to hell.

But as is usually the case during a time of transition, the pendulum has swung past the point of balance. While we have been consumed by *context*, the *content* of what we invest in students has taken a backseat. Most of us have spent little time determining what our students need to know before they graduate from high school. Our days are spent planning activities and designing camp T-shirts. Often the core of what we want students to learn gets lost in the shuffle.

Think for a moment about the class of students you just graduated from your ministry. What are the four or five key concepts, principles, or lessons you believe they walked away with as a result of their time under your leadership? As you consider that list, ask yourself: Are these the principles you set out years ago to instill in the hearts of the students under your watch? Or did they pick them up by chance?

The Ever-Raging Battle

Our students are being raised in an entertainment-oriented culture. Just about every morsel of relevant or irrelevant information they pick up is being served to them on a platter designed to stimulate the senses. If it doesn't entertain them, they aren't interested.

This is why so many of us have rushed to create high energy, entertainment-driven contexts for our ministries. And so we should—as long as the content doesn't suffer. But it is hard to stay content-focused when the "show" takes up so much time and energy.

How do we keep substance in the driver's seat? What can we do to keep the music from drowning out the message? How do we ensure that our students walk away from our youth ministries equipped to enter the next important stage of their lives?

Context vs. Content

This book is not about context. This book is about substance. It is about content. This book is about *what* you should communicate to your students, not *how* to communicate it. It is about instilling timeless principles into the hearts of teenagers to better equip them to live in their ever-changing culture.

Most youth leaders struggle with a lack of direction when it comes to the substance or content they are investing in their students. If you are like me, dozens and dozens of marketing pieces advertising new curriculums or teaching materials come across your desk every year. It is not that there is a lack of resources for teaching. It's that there is no systematic plan that lays out for us ahead of time the "irreducible minimum" around which to plan our teaching and curriculum choices.

Timeless Methods

We have a tendency to plan our environments and events first and *then* decide the content or substance to be taught. By adapting our ministries to the seven foundational truths presented in this book, however, we can turn that around. We can allow the truth of God's Word to dictate how we plan and create our environments and events. We often talk about the need to preserve the message while adjusting our methods to reach a new generation of students. We say we want to use what is cultural to communicate what is timeless. But in our attempts to remain methodologically relevant, many of us have dropped the ball when it comes to being intentional about the message.

Think about the time and energy you spend planning the context versus the content for a summer camp or youth retreat. Isn't it true that you tend to spend the majority of your time planning the right environment while leaving the content up to a guest speaker, someone who doesn't even know your kids?

What about your Bible study? You have chairs in rows (sometimes circles) for the students and a lectern for you or your assigned teacher. Perhaps you have doughnuts and juice on one table and quiet-time guides, event brochures, and announcement sheets on another. Your adult youth leaders stand on the back wall or sit in the last row of chairs. You plan the environment to a T, then you trust a publishing company to provide a lesson for you to teach. You have no idea what the lesson plan will be from one quarter to the next. The publisher decides what your students should learn, not you!

Of course we leave room for the Holy Spirit to move, and we trust the speakers and the writers. But perhaps the reason we "trust" other people so much is because *we're* not sure what we want our students to remember, understand, and apply.

If the truth were told, what have become foundational for us are our *methods*, not our content. We have slowly and unwittingly put the proverbial cart before the horse, and the results sit in our pews every Sunday morning in the shape of young adults who have a what's-in-it-for-me attitude and a weak biblical footing.

A Different Strategy

The leadership team of our student ministry at North Point Community Church in Alpharetta, Georgia, has invested many hours developing a ministry strategy that would be content-driven. What has evolved from our hard work is a ministry model that allows us to create environments based upon seven key biblical principles, or "checkpoints" as we refer to them.

Content drives our context. We are committed to creating relevant environments. But the environment must support the content. We have discovered that once we have identified *what* we want students to walk away with, creating the right environment is much easier. Our environments are more focused and effective.

This approach to student ministry does not de-emphasize the importance of a creative, fun, and relevant environment. Just the opposite is true. Once we have clarified what it is we want to communicate, we feel even more compelled to create just the right setting.

After all, it is one thing to put together a summer camp. It is quite another thing to create the optimal five-day environment for teenagers to rethink their whole approach to friendship. It is one thing to organize a winter retreat. But the stakes get higher when the goal is to create the optimal setting for students to examine their attitude toward the authorities God has placed in their lives. It is one thing to plan a quarter's worth of Sunday school curriculum. But what if the goal that quarter is to motivate students to adopt an others-first approach to relationships?

When content is the focus, the context becomes vitally important. This approach to youth ministry will motivate you and your leadership to raise the bar programmatically. Camp is camp. Sunday school is Sunday school. But what if these regularly scheduled events were viewed by your leadership as the context for imparting seven life-changing biblical principles? Suddenly the stakes are higher. Now camp, Sunday school, and the winter retreat are necessary means to a predetermined end.

Good Intentions

The seven checkpoints are an intentional, systematic approach to student discipleship focused on the *content* of discipleship. These seven student-specific principles are the irreducible minimum—the must-know, can't-be-without principles. They are not all that is important. But they are what is most important for students. I am convinced that these are the seven basic principles every student should understand, commit to memory, and embrace before they leave the safety of their homes and youth ministries.

As you begin your journey through the pages of this book, you will find that each of the seven checkpoints is restated in a powerful, easy-to-remember "Principle" of truth. Each checkpoint asks a "Critical Question," which helps you to evaluate your students based upon that principle, and includes a "Key Passage" from the Bible that serves as the timeless foundation for the principle. Finally, each checkpoint ends with a "Checking In" section to help you think about how each principle applies not only to your students' lives, but to your life as well.

The overall scope of the seven checkpoints looks like this:

Checkpoint #1: Authentic Faith

This checkpoint focuses on a correct understanding of faith. Confusion in this one area is the primary reason so many students abandon Christianity. True faith is confidence that God is who He says He is—and confidence that He will do everything He has promised to do.

Principle: God can be trusted; He will do all He has promised to do.

Critical Question: Are your students trusting God with the critical areas of their lives?

Key Passage: Proverbs 3:5–6

Checkpoint #2: Spiritual Disciplines

The focus of this checkpoint is your students' devotional life. The apostle Paul says that true spiritual transformation begins with a renewed mind. Only as teenagers begin to renew their minds according to the truths of Scripture will their attitudes and behavior begin to change.

Principle: When you see as God sees, you will do as God says.

Critical Question: Are your students developing a consistent devotional and prayer life?

Key Passage: Romans 12:2

Checkpoint #3: Moral Boundaries

One of the most important things you can teach your teenagers to do is to establish clear moral limits. They need to learn how to protect their bodies and emotions by honoring God's plan for sex and morality. That's the focus of this checkpoint. The depth of their intimacy with God and others is dependent upon it.

Principle: *Purity paves the way to intimacy.*

Critical Question: *Are your students establishing and maintaining godly moral boundaries?*

Key Passage: *1 Thessalonians 4:3–8*

Checkpoint #4: Healthy Friendships

The people your students associate with the most will have a direct impact on the decisions they make and the standards they choose. Healthy friendships build them up and draw them closer to God; unhealthy friendships bring them down and cause them to compromise what they know is right. This principle focuses on helping students build healthy friendships while avoiding unhealthy ones.

Principle: *Your friends will determine the direction and quality of your life.*

Critical Question: *Are your students establishing healthy friendships and avoiding unhealthy ones?*

Key Passage: *Proverbs 13:20*

Checkpoint #5: Wise Choices

This principle focuses on the necessity of applying godly wisdom to the choices students make. Good decision making is more than simply choosing between right and wrong. Teenagers need to learn to ask, "In light of my past experience and my future dreams, what is the wise thing for me to do in this situation?"

Principle: *Walk wisely.*

Critical Question: *Are your students making wise choices in every area of their lives?*

Key Passage: *Ephesians 5:15–17*

Checkpoint #6: Ultimate Authority

Teenagers often view freedom and authority as opposing concepts. But the Bible teaches that true freedom is found under authority. This principle focuses on students' need to recognize God's ultimate authority and respect the earthly authorities He has placed over them.

Principle: *Maximum freedom is found under God's authority.*

Critical Question: *Are your students submitting to the authorities God has placed over them?*

Key Passage: *Romans 13:1–2*

Checkpoint #7: Others First

Selfishness comes naturally to teenagers (not to mention the rest of us!) *Selflessness,* however, must be learned. The Bible says that Jesus "made himself nothing" in order to serve the people He loved. He put the needs of others ahead of His own. This checkpoint focuses on the true nature of humility and service.

Principle: *Consider others before yourself.*

Critical Question: *Are your students putting the needs of others ahead of their own?*

Key Passage: *Philippians 2:3–11*

Common Concerns

By this time you may be wondering, "Are you expecting me to teach these same seven concepts over and over?" Yes. I am suggesting that you develop all of your teaching environments and curriculums around the seven checkpoints. I know it doesn't sound feasible on the surface, but it is.

Repetition

When we present the seven-checkpoints strategy in seminars, leaders often question the wisdom of repeating the same things over and over. The concern is that repeating the same principles year after year spells doom for keeping students' interest in the things of God. True, repetition can lead to boredom over time. But the assumption is that repetition is the reason students get bored. In most cases the problem is not the repetition; it's the *presentation.*

It has been my experience that two things cause boredom in teenagers: a lifeless presentation by a teacher and the attempt to cover too much information in a short amount of time. Repetition has little to do with it. Rather, repetition is one of the main ways we learn. My coauthor, Stuart Hall, has a five-year-old son who recently learned how to kneeboard behind a jet ski. He didn't accomplish this feat on the first try. It took an hour of repeated instruction from his dad: "Lean back...extend your arms...shift your weight...." Now he skims across the water with a huge smile on his face. It was repetition that brought success.

I have never met a student who, after hearing one talk or

lesson on trusting God, fully understood the depths of that issue and obeyed the Lord for the rest of his or her life. Repetition has never hurt anyone, but it *has* transformed many lives spiritually, emotionally, and physically. You don't need to fear repetition!

Curriculum

One of the other concerns that is voiced from time to time is, Where are we going to find enough material on these seven topics to fill out a four- or six-year curriculum menu? Actually, that will not be as difficult as you might imagine. I wondered the same thing.

What I discovered is that once our team established a grid for the content of our student ministry, we knew exactly what curriculums to look for. Once we narrowed the focus, we were surprised to find how much material has been written on these seven common themes.

In addition to using published material, we have had success developing some of our own curriculums. Again, once we established the basic subject matter, it wasn't difficult to recruit several of our seasoned teachers to begin developing lesson plans. You may be surprised how eager your leadership will be to help fill the gaps in your curriculum menu once you give them some basic parameters.

Using the Checkpoints

We cycle the seven checkpoints through our middle-school and high-school ministry annually. As we plan our year, we look at the following four environments and ask the question, Which of the checkpoints would be best communicated in each of these settings?

Small Groups

Chances are you have some type of small group environment for your students. At North Point, our small group ministry for high-school students is called Inside Out. Inside Out meets on Sunday afternoons. Extreme, our small group environment for middle-school students, meets on Sunday mornings. In each of these environments a master teacher uses the first twenty minutes to focus the entire group on the checkpoint that is being discussed for the month.[1] Students then break up into small groups to discuss the checkpoint more personally and in detail. The small group leaders focus on facilitating discussion and applying truth rather than teaching the principle.

The goal of Inside Out and Extreme is for students to walk away with one concept and one point of application in their heads. By focusing on one principle, students are more apt to grasp and *apply* truth instead of merely *hearing* truth.

Outreach

In addition to small groups, you probably have created a weekly or monthly outreach environment. If you are successful, this is the setting your students feel most comfortable involving their unchurched friends in.

Our high-school outreach event happens on Wednesday

nights. It is called Rush Hour. At Rush Hour we take the same checkpoint we are discussing on Sundays and develop a talk for unchurched kids. Then we gear our entire presentation—video, music, drama, comedy, interaction with the speaker—to effectively communicate *one truth* to every student attending. Core students are then strongly encouraged to talk with their friends about what was communicated, and if appropriate, to invite them to Inside Out the following Sunday. In this way we use our midweek program to transition students into our small-group ministry.

Camps and Retreats

As we look at our ministry year, we use the seven checkpoints to determine the themes for our camps and retreats. By building our camps around one checkpoint, we know that our students will have at least one entire weekend or week per year totally devoted to that principle. For example, Vertical Reality, our fall retreat, always focuses on checkpoint #2, Spiritual Disciplines. We have found that this weekend-retreat setting is optimal for reinforcing spiritual disciplines in the lives of our high-school students, and we program contextually based on the content of the weekend.

There are several advantages to choosing a single checkpoint for a camp or weekend retreat. To begin with, once you have identified the focus of your content, you can be strategic in your selection of a camp speaker. Secondly, everybody on your planning team can have a sense of direction for worship, breakout groups, and devotional material. Lastly, you can clearly and succinctly communicate to parents the message you will be teaching their kids. How motivated would parents be to make sure their kids were signed up for camp if you announced that the theme was "Developing and Maintaining Healthy Friendships"? Imagine their excitement when you explain that the principle you hope to instill in their teenagers' hearts is *their friends have the potential to determine the direction and quality of their lives.*

Service Projects

A third environment that is conducive to reinforcing the seven checkpoints are service projects—mission trips, community service events, backyard Bible clubs, and so on. At North Point we use these types of environments to focus our student's attention on checkpoint #7, Others First.

Our primary others-first environment is a program called Student Impact. Student Impact is designed as an experiential learning environment that gives students the opportunity to discover their gifts and then use their gifts to serve our church on Sunday mornings.

By serving as small-group leaders for preschoolers, elementary age children, or middle schoolers, our high-school students put others first every Sunday morning. They also serve on various worship and production teams. As part of Student Impact, they are required to participate in ongoing training that is designed to help them understand their responsibility to put others first through the use of their gifts and the investment of their time.

Total Integration

As youth ministers a generation apart in age and living miles apart geographically, Stuart and I both focused our teaching for most of our respective years in youth ministry on the irreducible minimum represented in this book. We each discovered separately the value of focusing and refocusing the minds and hearts of our students on a handful of principles that would prepare them for the next stage in their lives. Unfortunately, neither of us had the ability to integrate these seven essentials into the overall framework of our respective student ministries.

Now working together at North Point Community Church, we have taken the seven-checkpoints concept to the next level. Thanks to the vision and leadership of our family minister, Reggie Joiner; our director of student ministry, Kevin Ragsdale; and our middle-school director, Heath Bennett; these seven principles have become the core curriculum for all of our student-oriented environments. Content is truly driving our context. And nobody is complaining about the repetition.

Making an Impact

When you signed on for youth ministry, producing events and shuffling papers were the last things you had in mind. You wanted then, as you do now, to make a difference in the lives of teenagers. But it probably wasn't long before you found yourself drowning in a sea of paperwork and administrative duties. If you are wired anything like me, by the time you get your summer camp organized, you're not even sure you want to go!

Meanwhile, kids are coming and going. Growing up. Breaking up. Graduating. Moving on. Chances are, as busy as you might have been during their tenure in your youth ministry, they will never forget you. But surely you want them to remember more than just you! You didn't respond to God's call to youth ministry so *you* would be remembered. You signed on to shape the attitudes and beliefs of a generation. You responded to this call for the sake of the one kid you might help avoid the mistakes you made when you were a teenager.

I believe the principles embodied in the seven checkpoints are essential to the relational, emotional, and spiritual health of our teenagers. You touch on most of these topics from time to time anyway. Why not embrace a plan that will help you integrate these seven core ideas into everything you are doing in your ministry?

When we were preparing this manuscript, Stuart told me a story that I think illustrates the impact we all want to make on at least a handful of the students God entrusts to our care. It shows what can happen when a youth minister refuses to settle for simply being remembered:

> Kellee and I had been married exactly one year when we agreed to move from Mobile, Alabama, to Bossier City, Louisiana. I had taken a position as minister to students at First Baptist Church of Bossier City. We were there for five wonderful years.
>
> About four months after starting in Bossier, we met

Kevin. Kevin's parents are not wealthy by any stretch of the imagination. He has a younger brother who is autistic. Kevin has since admitted to me that he always struggled with not being proud of his family and upbringing. He never owned the most fashionable clothes. People always made fun of him. In the world's view of things, Kevin was born without much of a chance to succeed in life.

Kevin came to church every Sunday on the church bus. It never failed that I would have the daunting task of rounding up Kevin and his friends as they tried weekly to skip church and start trouble.

One Sunday in Cross Training, our student Bible study on Sunday mornings, Kevin and his cohorts were sitting directly behind Kellee and making too much noise. When Kellee turned and nicely asked Kevin to quiet down, he introduced her to an array of filthy curse words that would make Chris Rock sound like Mother Teresa.

Unfortunately, it cost Kevin his weekly trip to our church for a month. Those bus drivers did not play!

Slowly but surely Kevin began to change. Some of our students befriended him, and he became an active part of the student ministry. God started transforming his life, and I had the privilege of watching Kevin grow spiritually.

Kevin made the varsity football team at Airline High School, and it was always a blast to watch Kevin pace the sidelines every Friday night. He was always the consummate team player, and his teammates could count on his encouragement and support. Although he rarely stepped foot on the field, he had the heart of a champion.

Kevin spent many weekends at my house during his senior year. He was honest about his struggles. He was burdened for his friends. He made me laugh with his stories about how the girl of his dreams would never give in to his romantic attempts to win her heart. He was so hungry to know God in a deeper way.

I must admit there were times when his knock at my door made my head drop, but I never regretted the hours I spent with him. I would always walk away from those times so grateful for the fact that God had allowed Kevin to enter my life. Little did I know that my efforts to help Kevin understand authentic faith, practice spiritual disciplines, establish moral boundaries, develop meaningful friendships, make wise choices, submit to God-given authority, and think of others before himself would make such a lasting impression on his life.

After graduation, Kevin decided to attend Louisiana State University in Baton Rouge. During his four years at LSU, he mentored junior-high students at the church he attended, played rugby, and was a volunteer football coach for University High School while being the ultimate Tiger football fan.

When he informed me that he planned to major in pre-law, I must admit that I laughed deep down.

I'm not laughing anymore.

Kevin graduated with a perfect 4.0 average. Through all four years of college—majoring in pre-law!

He has been accepted to law school at Harvard University and starts this fall. His desire is to become a lawyer and give most of what he earns to furthering the gospel of Christ.

Stuart concluded his story with this remark: "Kevin is just one of the reasons I believe in these seven principles. But he is a great reason."

I couldn't agree more.

Checking In
Read 1 and 2 Timothy
Think about It

Would you consider your ministry effective? Why or why not? Look at your calendar and daily schedule. What consumes most of your time? Are those things making your ministry more effective? _____

_____

_____

_____

_____

If a parent were to walk into your office today and ask what principles you intend to invest in his or her child, could you give a clear and defined answer? What would you say?

_____

_____

_____

_____

_____

_____

Think back to the last four summer camps or retreats you have done. What were the themes and principles taught at those camps?_____

_____

_____

_____

_____

_____

Highlight those places in 1 and 2 Timothy where you see Paul instilling one of the seven checkpoint principles in Timothy's life. Mark each place with the checkpoint number.

_____

Why do you think Paul was repetitious in his discipleship of Timothy?_____

_____

_____

_____

_____

If you were to adopt the seven checkpoints in this book, what would be the greatest roadblock in your church for implementing them?_____

_____

_____

_____

What's It All About?: The Seven Checkpoints

Journal any thoughts, questions, or comments you have after reading this introduction. _____

_____

_____

_____

_____

_____

_____

_____

_____

_____

_____

_____

_____

_____

Checkpoint #1

Authentic Faith
Putting Your Trust in God

Principle

God can be trusted; He will do all He has promised to do.

Critical Question

Are your students trusting God with the critical areas of their lives?

Key Passage

Proverbs 3:5–6

I'm the first one to admit
that I am somewhat cynical
when it comes to faith.
I envy people
who can just let go and
totally commit.
I, on the other hand,
can't even hear the title
of the show
Touched by an Angel
without thinking that a
professional baseball player is
being sued for sexual harassment.

—DENNIS MILLER
in his book *I Rant, Therefore I Am*

#1

Authentic Faith
Putting Your Trust in God

As Christians we are instructed to live by faith. But what does that mean—especially when it comes to Christian teenagers in the twenty-first century? What exactly is faith? Believe me, today's students want to know!

If they have a whole lot of faith, does that mean that God will answer all of their prayers? Why does their faith go down the tubes when things go bad?

Faith is the critical, foundational element in the process of spiritual renewal and growth. For that reason it is imperative that the students in our youth ministries understand what faith is and what it isn't. Unfortunately, confusion over the definition of faith is rampant in the greater Christian community. Often faith is spoken of as if it is some kind of force or power—something we can turn on when we need it if only we can find the right switch. But that's a faulty definition of faith.

Confusion in this one area is the primary reason so many students abandon Christianity. It is the reason they have such difficulty trusting God with every area of their lives. It is also the reason so many are unsure of their salvation. Conference after conference, meeting after meeting, camp after camp, they raise their hand again to indicate that they are receiving Christ as their Savior. They're not sure it "took" the last time.

Shattered Faith

Like me, you probably know students who would readily admit that they *used to be* Christians. They *used to* go to church, but not anymore. They *used to* believe, but not anymore. They have "lost" their faith.

Two factors more than anything else are responsible for shattering the faith of young people. The first is *poor choices*. When "believing" students veer off course morally, relationally, or ethically, they are immediately confronted with a tidal wave of guilt. And there are only two ways they can get rid of guilt: ask for forgiveness and change their behavior or change their belief system. If students can convince themselves that there is nothing wrong with what they are doing, their guilt is greatly diminished. Changing how they believe is often easier than changing how they behave.

Many "used-to-believe" students decided at some point to trade in their faith for a more convenient lifestyle. What does that say about their faith? Obviously, it had shallow roots. It was based on convenience rather than conviction. Their faith was rooted in the present, on what worked for them at the time. It could be summarized this way:

> **What's happening now,**
> **What I'm feeling now,**
> **Determines what I believe for now.**

The second factor that often undermines faith is *unexplainable tragedy*—painful or adverse circumstances that don't "fit" with the students' understanding of the character of God or the Christian faith. When students are confronted with tragedy, they ask, "How could a good God allow this to happen? Why didn't He stop it?"

The inability to figure out why a good God would allow bad things to happen has caused many teenagers to abandon Christianity. Like their friends who made poor choices, their faith proved to be shallow and rooted in the present. The mantra of their faith is the same:

> **What's happening now,**
> **What I'm feeling now,**
> **Determines what I believe for now.**

As long as our students' faith is grounded in what they see and experience, their faith will always be fragile. It will never be more than circumstantial faith—totally dependent upon their ability (or inability) to interpret the events and circumstances around them.

Interpretation, Please

Let's say sixteen-year-old Kim prays and prays for God to help her pass a test—but she fails. So Kim interprets that failure to mean that God doesn't answer prayer. Or maybe He is mad at her. She concludes that God can't be trusted. Her faith is shattered by her interpretation of the circumstances.

Of course we are all prone to misinterpret events. It's not just a teenage problem! Ask a four-year-old being carried by his father into the doctor's office if Daddy loves him. When the doctor brandishes a needle for a tetanus shot, the little boy might have his doubts.

But years later, ask that same child about the doctor's visit. He will have a completely different perspective. He will know that his father showed his love by caring enough to protect his son's health.

Just as a child cannot correctly judge his parent's character based upon one scary trip to the doctor, so we dare not draw conclusions about God's goodness based upon the immediate circumstances of life. God's faithfulness and loving character are never predicated upon the unfolding of circumstances.

Circumstantial faith is fragile because its frame of reference is too small. Teenagers have an especially hard time judging the significance of current events in the context of a lifetime, much less weighing out those events on the scale of eternity. They can't see past the ever-changing landscape of their immediate surroundings. If God doesn't answer their prayers by next week, they wonder if He exists. If they don't see God at work in their present situations, they lose their confidence in His love and care for them. Instead they get stressed out over things like taking a test, getting a date, winning a game, or being left off a party list. Neutrogena and Oxy10 are making a killing off of them!

Authentic faith looks at the whole picture. We need to remind our students about Joseph, who spent fifteen years as a slave in Egypt after being sold into slavery by his own brothers. His "tragedy" was a part of a beautiful tapestry that God was weaving behind the scenes to save an entire region from famine. Then there was Moses, who spent forty years in the wilderness before God sent him back to Egypt—freeing a nation from slavery and unfolding a wonderful purpose in his seemingly purposeless existence.

The problem for our students is simply a faulty understanding of faith. As leaders, our job is to help them replace that faulty understanding with an authentic faith that is properly grounded.

The Foundation of Faith

The foundation of Christian faith, of course, is a person, not a circumstance. We must redirect our students' faith away from current events and help them fasten it upon Jesus Christ, the only one in whom they can securely place their trust.

I like to refer the students in my youth ministry to the Book of Hebrews, which was written to a group of Christians who were being pressured by their community—and tough circumstances in general—to abandon their faith. The author of Hebrews encouraged his readers to keep believing on the basis of the *identity of Christ*. In the first three chapters he presented a mountain of evidence pointing toward the conclusion that Christ is God. We can believe, he declared, because we know that Jesus walked on this earth, claimed to be God, gave evidence supporting His claim, died for our sin, rose from the dead, and went back to heaven in plain view of hundreds of witnesses. He concluded by stating, "Therefore, since we have a great high priest who has gone through the heavens, Jesus the Son of God, let us hold firmly to the faith we profess."[1]

Our students must base their faith on the identity of Christ. If Christ really is who He says He is, then they don't need to worry when bad things happen to them. They have a high priest who understands. If Jesus really died for their sins, then they have no reason to doubt His love. They have a friend who has laid down His life for them. And if He really meant it when He promised to come back for them, then they don't have to be afraid of what happens next in life. They have a heavenly Father who has their best interests in mind!

If our students' faith rests on anything other than the person of Jesus Christ—who He is and what He has done for them—they are building their lives upon a fragile foundation. Eventually the choices of life will sway them to adapt or compromise what they believe. Circumstances will cause them to doubt God. But God never intended for their faith to rest upon what's going on around them.

The foundation of their faith must be the person of Jesus Christ. And we have the responsibility to lead them to this conclusion! If we can help our students understand the significance of building the foundation of their faith on Jesus, then we are securing them to an immovable object. Their faith will not be swayed by the circumstances of life.

Faith Undefined

You wouldn't know it from talking to a lot of teenagers, but faith is actually a very simple concept. Then why are so many students confused? The answer is also simple: People tend to be unwilling to accept faith for what it really is rather than what they want it to be. They want faith to be a power that moves God in a direction they have prescribed. They want it to be the code that unlocks the door to God's unlimited resources—resources they can use at their discretion. Basically, they want faith to be a way for them to get what they want from God.

This way of thinking is so ingrained in the minds of students that when God says no to a request, they have a difficult time taking no for an answer. They assume that there is either something wrong with them or something wrong with Him. You and I both know students who have abandoned their faith altogether because God wouldn't cooperate. They believed God was obligated to act on their faith. When He didn't, they walked away from the whole thing.

Our students need to understand that biblical faith is not a *force* or a *power*. It is not something to tap into. It is not a tool to get something from God. Obi Wan Kenobi ("May the force be with you") is not the leader! That sort of thinking comes dangerously close to New Age philosophy and has no basis in the Bible.

Nor is biblical faith merely *confidence*. When a basketball team bursts out of the locker room pumped up for a game, those players believe they are going to win. If you were to ask the fans in the bleachers if they have faith in their team, they would shout, "Yes!" But that's not biblical faith. That's confidence. Many students think that if they muster up enough confidence, God will act. They don't realize that faith and confidence are not the same thing.

Biblical faith is also not *wishful thinking*. When students wish for something, they want it, but they have no guarantee that they will get it.

Faith Defined

According to the author of Hebrews, "faith is being sure of what we hope for and certain of what we do not see."[2] You can look at it this way. If you wrote me and invited me to meet with your leadership team, would you have faith that I was coming? Would you announce it to your church? No. You may wish I would come, but you wouldn't have faith that I would come. What would it take for you to have faith that I was coming? You would need a letter or phone call confirming the fact that I had accepted your invitation. You would need a promise from me that I will be there. The promise would allow you to move from wishful thinking to faith.

The bridge from wishful thinking to faith is the revelation

of God—the wonderful promises He gives to us in His Word. Our students don't need to merely wish that He would have their best interests in mind; they can be absolutely confident that He does!

I've come up with the following working definition of authentic faith: *Faith is confidence that God is who He says He is and that He will do all He has promised to do.* Our students' confidence can't be in themselves or their friends or their circumstances (or even their youth pastor). Each of these will eventually let them down. Their confidence must be in the absolute promises and the unchanging character of God.

In Hebrews 11, the author gives dozens of illustrations of people who showed authentic biblical faith. In every case that faith was grounded in a promise or a revelation from God. Noah spent 140 years building an ark because God promised that it was going to rain. Abraham left his home and set out without a destination in mind because God promised to lead him to a new home. Gideon charged into an enemy camp totally outnumbered because God promised victory. Moses went back to Egypt and confronted Pharaoh because God promised to deliver Israel through him. Joshua marched around Jericho until the walls fell down because God promised success.

What will our students be capable of doing when they begin to live by authentic faith—when they are completely confident that God is who He says He is and that He will do what He has promised to do? It's exciting to think about!

Who's in Charge?

Unfortunately, students often resist this definition of faith. Let's face it: We all want to be in the driver's seat. There is something inside each of us that wants a "faith" that puts us in control. I know I wrestled with this issue as a high-school student. I was always trying to find a way, a gimmick, a magic prayer that would force God to do my bidding. But biblical faith puts God firmly in control of our lives. Authentic faith leaves Him with the option to say no.

Our students must understand this distinction. Only when they come to terms with the true nature of faith will they be able to surrender their will to God's. The outcome of authentic faith is a life that is in alignment with the will of the Father. As long as they are trying to get something *from* God, they will have a difficult time surrendering their lives *to* God.

The Good Father

One of the best things we can do for our students is to consistently present God as a perfect father. As my friend Louie Giglio is fond of saying, "God is not a *reflection* of our earthly fathers; He is the *perfection* of our earthly fathers." Jesus Himself instructed us to address God as "Father." He could have chosen any of a dozen Old Testament analogies for us to use. But He chose "Father," and that is how we must present God to our students. It is the only paradigm that is consistent with biblical faith.

Because God is a perfect Father, students can ask Him for anything they desire. Jesus assured us that God loves to give good gifts to His children who ask.[3] We see this love illustrated repeatedly in the Gospels. Often when Jesus healed the blind and the lame, He admonished them not to tell anyone what had happened to them. Apparently, Jesus healed these people simply because He, like His Father, enjoyed giving good things to those He loved. Jesus had no personal agenda. His gifts were not a means to an end. He gave because He enjoyed giving.

Still, as a perfect Father, God would not dare give His children everything they ask for. He knows that many things teenagers think they want so badly are simply not good for them—in fact, some are downright dangerous to their spiritual lives. But because He is a perfect Father, they can always trust Him—even when He seems to act out of character or they don't understand what He's doing. Even when He says no!

Promises, Promises

Our heavenly Father can be trusted to do all He has promised to do. In teaching our students about faith, then, it is important that we distinguish between what God has and has not promised.

Earlier in this chapter I noted that tragedy is often behind the demise of a student's faith. But the underlying cause is actually unmet expectations. Let's say that Rick, a ninth grader, prays that God will not let his parents divorce. As he prays, his expectations increase. And as his expectations increase, his "faith" increases. Then Dad walks in and announces that Mom has filed for divorce. Rick is devastated.

"What's the point in praying?" he wonders. "Where is God? Why would He let me down like this?"

As youth ministers we must address this and similar kinds of situations all the time. There are no easy answers. In fact there are *no* answers in the moments following such heavy blows. But a proper understanding of faith provides a safe context for dealing with life's disappointments.

The last thing Rick needs to feel in his time of crisis is isolation from God. On the contrary, this is a time when he needs to cling to God more than ever before! Yet his expectations and "faith" have set him up for disappointment with God. And as a result, he feels like he must handle his disappointment alone, without God.

We must help our students learn to distinguish between God's promises and their own expectations. There are many things God has not promised that they might wish He had. God has not promised to keep bad things from happening to them, for example. He has not promised to heal every illness. He has not promised to reverse the consequences of sin. Yet there are occasions when God intervenes and does all of these things. Why? Because He is a good God who loves to give good gifts to His children.

But these are not promises. He is under no obligation. And the fact that parents divorce and grandparents die and friends move away is no reflection on the goodness or the presence of our heavenly Father.

One of the best ways we can help students make these distinctions is to point them to the experiences of the apostles.

These were certainly men of great faith. Yet their lives were not free from difficulty. God didn't always intervene. But an answer of no did not undermine their faith. They understood that the foundation of their faith was not always getting the answer they wanted. It was not their ability to figure out what God was up to. Their faith was grounded in a risen Savior.

Count on It

So what can teenagers expect from God? What has He promised? Again, the writer of Hebrews helps us out by identifying the two things students can always expect. See if you can spot them:

> Therefore, since we have a great high priest who has gone through the heavens, Jesus the Son of God, let us hold firmly to the faith we profess. For we do not have a high priest who is unable to sympathize with our weaknesses, but we have one who has been tempted in every way, just as we are—yet was without sin. Let us then approach the throne of grace with confidence, so that we may receive mercy and find grace to help us in our time of need.[4]

Our students need to understand that because Jesus is their high priest, they can draw near to God with confidence. Many will respond, "Confidence in what? I already know that He may not give me what I want. He might say no. How can I ask for anything with confidence?" But they *can* have confidence that God will always give them the two things that are most critical in their time of need: *mercy* and *grace*.

Have Mercy!

Mercy comes in many forms. Sometimes it is simply the comfort students feel from knowing that, in some mysterious way, they have God's undivided attention when they pour their hearts out to Him. At times mercy comes in the form of physical or emotional relief. Mercy is the assurance that God will never allow the pressures or heartbreaks of life to be more than they can bear.

When I teach this principle to the students in my youth ministry, I assure them that their Savior knows far more about what they are experiencing than they think He does. To prove it I take them on a journey through Christ's own experiences. Jesus is able to enter into their pain and understand how they feel, I explain, because He also knew:

- ✔ *Temptation.* He experienced temptation at the hand of Satan himself.

- ✔ *Rejection.* He was rejected by both friends and family members.

- ✔ *Failure.* He saw everything He had lived for and worked for crumble around Him.

- ✔ *Fear.* In the Garden of Gethsemene, He spent an entire night dreading the events of the next day.

- ✔ *Abandonment.* His friends ran away when He needed them most.

- ✔ *Loneliness.* He even faced death alone.

My point is that the students have a Savior who under-stands. He has felt what they feel. Therefore, He knows exactly what they need. They can come boldly to God with total trans-parency and openness, confident that He will never say, "I can't believe you did that." Or, "I can't believe you feel that way." Or, "What is your problem?" He is a mercy-giving God because He knows from experience what it is like to need mercy.

Hang On

But God's promises don't end with mercy. Students can expect to receive grace as well. In this context "grace" means the strength to endure, the ability to carry on. Mom may never understand. Dad may never come back. A teacher may never lighten up. Popularity may always be elusive. The schol-arship may never come through. But God has promised to give grace. He has not promised to deliver them *from* their cir-cumstances; He has promised to deliver them *through* them. Students have the freedom to ask their heavenly Father to change their circumstances—and they can count on Him for the grace to endure in the meantime.

Saving Faith

When I was a kid I must have asked Jesus to come into my heart a thousand times. Salvation to me was like a bad cold; I wanted to make sure I "got it."

I remember the time an evangelist preached about "head faith" versus "heart faith." Head faith, he said, wasn't enough.

You had to believe in your heart. After all, even the devil believes in his head! So I prayed again for heart faith—just in case I still didn't have the real thing.

I know my experience is not unique. I talk to students all the time who have "prayed the prayer" over and over and still aren't sure if they are "saved." This confusion stems from a general misunderstanding about the nature of faith. Many students have the notion that the *quality* of their faith is an issue with God. So they pray for salvation and wonder if they "really" believed or believed "enough" or believed "in their hearts." When that misunderstanding is combined with the emphasis many church leaders put on "praying the prayer," it is no wonder the same kids keep getting "saved" year after year.

The essence of saving faith is simpler than that. In a nutshell, God has promised to forgive our sins once and for all if we put our trust in Christ's death as the payment for those sins. That's it. That's the gospel.

When students come to me doubting their salvation, I don't ask them if they have prayed to receive Christ. I ask them what they are trusting in to get them to heaven. Nearly every time they answer, "I am trusting in Jesus." To which I respond, "Then you are in!"

Having said it simply, let me try to confuse you now with more information.

The Facts about Faith

I always explain to my students that faith must have an object—typically a person or a product. If I told them that I was going to come to their house for dinner, the object of their faith would be me. If a bar of soap were advertised as being especially good for stopping breakouts, the object of their faith would be the bar of soap. The object of faith is *who* they believe or the *product* they believe in.

Furthermore, faith must always have *content*. When they believe in a product they believe something *about* the product. They believe it will do what it claims it will do—for example, that the soap will help keep pimples away. Similarly, if they believe in a person, they are confident that the person is trustworthy and will do what he says he will do. They believe, for example, that I will show up at their house if I say I will. The content of faith is what a person or product promises to do for them. It is *what* they believe.

Saving faith has a very specific object and a very specific content. The object of saving faith is Jesus—not just God. Jesus said, "I am the way and the truth and the life. No one comes to the Father except through me."[5]

But what specifically do students need to believe about Jesus? The content of saving faith is like a pair of concrete stakes that must be driven deep into their teenage hearts: (1) Jesus is the Son of God, and (2) His death on the cross paid the penalty for all of their sins—apart from anything they do or intend to do to try to "earn" their salvation.

Students can believe a multitude of other things about Christ. They can believe that He was born of a virgin, did miracles, died on a cross, and never sinned. The Bible says that each of these is true. But they are not the critical elements of saving faith. The problem with saving faith is not that it is so complex, but that it is so simple!

The way a person comes to salvation is through faith. If you were to ask your students next Sunday morning why they are at church, they would not answer, "Because of my car!" Their car would be the vehicle that got them to church, but it is not the reason they came. They came to please God and worship with fellow believers. Similarly, faith is the vehicle that carries us to salvation, but Jesus is the reason we are saved. We are saved *through* faith but not *because of* faith.

Salvation is a gift from God. It is not a reward gift. God does not offer it because we deserve it. God offers every person salvation because that is His desire.

The way students receive that free gift of salvation is through trusting in God's offer. That is saving faith. It is confidence that God is who He says He is and that He will do all He has promised to do. Students can rest in the fact that God saved them *by* grace *through* faith—just because He wanted to.

Follow the Leader

There is a promise attached to authentic faith. The writer of Proverbs describes it this way: "Trust in the LORD with all your heart and lean not on your own understanding; in all your ways acknowledge him, And he will make your paths straight."[6]

The challenge in this verse is one we need to bring to our students over and over again. They must trust in the Lord with all their hearts. That is, they must trust God with every area of their lives. He is a perfect Father who can be trusted.

And in response to that trust, He promises to give them guidance. Literally, God will make their path—their direction in life—clear and obvious.

I love what Thomas Merton said about God's guidance: "We receive enlightenment only in proportion as we give ourselves more and more completely to God by humble submission and love. We do not first see, and then act: we act, then see...and that is why the man who waits to see clearly before he will believe, never starts on the journey."[7]

If our students are going to trust in the Lord with all their hearts, they must be assured that God is trustworthy. We need to do everything in our power to provide them with the proper context for making that determination. It is up to us to remove the fog surrounding the issue of faith and to assure them that God is who He says He is—a perfect Father. And like a perfect Father, He will do everything He has promised to do and more.

Checking In
Read Hebrews 1–4 and 11:1
Think about It

Have you ever changed the way you believed about something?

_____

_____

_____

_____

_____

_____

Checkpoint #1: Authentic Faith

Have you ever decided that there was nothing wrong with something that you were doing and then changed the way you believed in order to soothe your conscience?

_____

_____

_____

_____

_____

Has tragedy ever caused you to doubt or lose faith in God? Explain. _____

_____

_____

_____

_____

_____

_____

_____

In your own words, define faith.

_____

_____

_____

_____

Reread Hebrews 4:14. Would you say that you hold firmly to your faith? Why or why not?

_____

_____

_____

_____

Make a list of all the evidences of Jesus identified in Hebrews 1–3. What does this evidence mean to you?

_____

_____

_____

_____

_____

_____

_____

In general, would you say that the faith of your students is more circumstance-focused than Christ-focused? Why or why not?

_____

_____

_____

_____

Checkpoint #2
Spiritual Disciplines
Seeing with God's Eyes

Principle

When you see as God sees, you will do as God says.

Critical Question

Are your students developing a consistent devotional and prayer life?

Key Passage

Romans 12:2

If you want to be somebody else,
if you're tired of losing battles
with yourself,
if you want to be somebody else,
change your mind.

—SISTER HAZEL
from their song "Change Your Mind"

Spiritual Disciplines
Seeing with God's Eyes

In the days of Christopher Columbus, the common belief was that the world was flat; if you sailed to the horizon, you would surely fall off the edge of the earth to your death. Columbus was contemplating this belief one day while sitting under a tree eating an orange. Suddenly a butterfly landed on top of the orange, and Columbus watched in wonder as the beautiful creature walked around and down the side of the orange without falling off.

A light bulb went off in his head. Columbus reasoned that the same force of nature that kept that butterfly connected to the underside of the orange would also keep him and his ship connected to the earth. We now know that it was actually microscopic "suction cups" on the pads of the butterfly's little feet that kept it stuck to the orange. But with this new perspective, Columbus was emboldened to sail past the horizon and discover a whole new world that we now call home.

The way we perceive things shapes our reality. This was certainly true for Columbus. This is also why the students in our youth ministries do most of the things they do. From matters of faith to relationships to service, perspective is what drives our students' behavior.

Our calling as youth leaders is clear: We are to do everything in our power to help our students get the right perspective—God's perspective. We need to help them see as God sees. If they can see things from God's perspective, they will be more likely to adapt their behavior to do what He says. Simple? Yes. Easy? No.

The Big D

The good news is that God has documented His take on all of life in the Bible. The bad news is that our students look to us to chop it up and feed it to them in bite-size morsels. It is the *discipline* of reading God's Word, understanding what He means, and doing what He says that students struggle with.

For the most part, *discipline* and *teenager* are mutually exclusive concepts. Aren't the teenage years designed for the sole purpose of practicing irresponsibility? Parents and youth leaders seem to accept bad habits and irresponsible behavior from students without batting an eye. It is what we have come to expect.

The same holds true when it comes to teenagers and *spiritual* disciplines. We have low expectations. But the ability or inability of our students to develop consistent spiritual disciplines will have a dramatic impact on the quality of their relationship with Christ, both now and in the long-term. We must lift our standard of discipline. So must they.

A Changed Life

Most teenagers would agree that becoming a Christian means that their lives should change. But they assume (along with many adults) that "praying the prayer" or making a commitment at the end of a church service or youth camp automatically results in lasting change. When they see no immediate or consistent difference in their lives, they begin to wonder about the reality of their faith.

But the Christian life doesn't work that way. Prayer is not a magic bullet guaranteeing change. Rededication is nothing more than a promise; it doesn't ensure the ability to follow through.

The apostle Paul put a different spin on change when he wrote, "Do not conform any longer to the pattern of this world, but be transformed by the renewing of your mind."[1] What brings about transformation or change? A *renewed mind.* But renewal is not instantaneous. It is a process of exchanging old for new, of taking off old things and putting on new things. In the context of our life in Christ, renewal is the process of removing lies and replacing them with truth. Students must remove the lies that have been inherent in their old ways of thinking and replace them one by one with the truths of God's Word.

Think about it. When students give their lives to Christ,

does God erase the insecurities and lustful thoughts that have harassed them for years? No. Those students wake up the next morning fighting the same stuff they battled the day before. Their identity is in Christ, but their mind is still full of crud. Their brains have to catch up with their new identity! That is why Paul is so emphatic—and why we must be too—when he says that true change can happen only when the mind is renewed.

Our students will never live transformed lives until they have transformed minds. They will never have transformed minds until they have God's thoughts. It is His perspective, His mind that students need to gain. And students will never gain God's thoughts until they begin to develop intimacy with Him by exercising the spiritual disciplines of time alone with God, Scripture memorization, journaling, and prayer.

Listen Up!

Students always seem to find the time to tell God what they need done or fixed in their lives. But how often do they give Him time to speak? I have never met a student whose problems stemmed from the fact that he or she didn't talk enough to God. However, I *have* counseled numerous students whose problems stemmed from the fact that they never developed the habit of listening to God. Most of these students' deepest regrets, I'm convinced, could have been avoided if they had only listened to God and obeyed His Word.

What's Your Priority?

Communication is a crucial element in any intimate relationship—including a relationship with God. And communication always involves listening.

Jesus understood this. Nowhere do we see the importance of communication with the Father better illustrated than in the life of Christ. In fact, Jesus' time alone with the Father was His ultimate priority. It took priority over ministry, family, friends, even sleep. Jesus refused to allow the tyranny of the urgent or the expectations of others to shape His agenda and schedule. As strange as it may sound, He put His own spiritual welfare ahead of the spiritual and physical welfare of others. He knew He would be of no help to them otherwise.

Jesus came to do the will of the Father. But in order to *do* the will of the Father, He had to *know* the will of the Father. That's why Jesus made it a priority to spend time alone with God—to know the One who sent Him.

Time alone with God must become our students' priority if they are serious about pursuing intimacy with Him. God wants to communicate to our teenagers, not just do things for them. And He *will* speak to them through His Word in a real and personal way if they will give Him an opportunity to do so.

So why don't they? Many students argue that they didn't realize they were *supposed* to spend time with God. Other students say that they don't know *how* to spend time with God. But I believe the main reason students don't spend intimate time alone with God is that they don't feel any *urgency* to do so.

Getting to school, practice, or work on time is urgent. Homework is urgent. But time alone with God generally doesn't fall into the same category. After all, if students miss a quiet time or two (or twenty), there is no immediate consequence. They don't get kicked off the team. They don't have to repeat a class. Nobody sends a letter to their parents.

But students who don't set aside time to listen to God *will* pay a price eventually. If they don't listen, they will not learn; and if they don't learn, they will not change. They won't develop intimacy with God. Instead, they will approach God as if He were a vending machine, with a "Give me, bless me, help me!" attitude. If students don't take time to listen to God, what began as a loving relationship with their heavenly Father will devolve into routine, ritual, and religion.

Developing a strong devotional life, however, will help students move from a religious approach to God to the relational approach He desires. If students have no intimate communication with God, He tends to get relegated to church buildings and days of the week. He becomes a duty. This religious approach is why so many students go to church every week but their lives never change. It is most often the reason why students who graduate from high school and leave our youth groups never darken the doors of a church again.

A strong devotional life is the one thing that will develop a sense of relationship and accountability between students and their heavenly Father. When students get into the habit of spending personal time alone with God, they enter into a new realm of accountability. To a teenager, all the difference in the world lies between hearing a preacher telling them what to do and sitting alone with the Bible and hearing the same thing from God Himself.

It's a Date

Obviously God can speak to our students whenever and wherever He wishes. But it's still important that they plan for a specific, scheduled time alone with God. In doing so they are not putting God in a box; rather, they are learning to prioritize their lives as Jesus did. They are developing a listening heart that is tuned to the voice of God.

We need to help students choose a time and place to listen. You and I both know that some environments are better for listening than others. When I need to tell my wife something important, there are certain environments I avoid. The dinner table is one. Loud restaurants are another. If you came to see me about something important, I wouldn't ask you to sit and talk in the church reception area. There are too many distractions. I would ask you to come into my office.

When it comes to listening to God, some environments are better than others. Jesus knew this. That's why He was always going off by Himself to the mountains, the wilderness, or the garden. Ideally, students need to find a place that they can use for the sole purpose of spending time alone with God—a place where they can focus on Him. It might be a guest room in their house. It might be a corner of their bedroom. It might be a particular chair in their living room. When I was in high school, I used to drive to a park before school and sit on a particular rock.

Some times are also better than others. If I want to talk to my wife about something important, I know I need to catch her before 10:30 P.M. Jesus often slipped away early in the morning to be alone with God. Apparently, that was an optimal listening time for Him.

The reason most students don't spend time alone with God is because they don't plan to. Yet students make dates for everything else in their cluttered lives. If they want to spend time with you, they call your office and schedule it, right? "Let's get together sometime" rarely gets anyone together. Students need to go to bed knowing when and where they are going to spend their time alone with God the next day. They need to think of this time as their appointment—their date— with their heavenly Father.

All by Myself

Think about the following people from the Bible: Abraham, Moses, Joshua, Jonah, David, John the Baptist, Paul, and Jesus. All of these men have a common thread in their history. Do you know what it is? God allowed each of them to go through an extended period of solitude before they began to influence the world. We often look at their solitude as a time of punishment, but God looked at their solitude as the perfect environment for transformation in their lives. He still approaches solitude the same way.

Intimacy with God is elusive to students because it hinges

on a fleeting component in their lives: *time*. The practice of solitude helps them capture time. It pushes out distraction and interruption, the two greatest enemies of intimacy. It slows down the clock. Whenever students can capture time through solitude, that is the best time for them to spend intimate moments with God.

As we noted, Jesus found that His best time was in the early morning.[2] Personally I think that early morning is the best time for students to spend time alone with God too. It is a practical way of applying the scripture "But seek *first* his kingdom and his righteousness."[3] Early morning solitude helps students to mentally and morally reboot their conscience and perspective. It clears out previous confusion. It allows them to pray through their schedule for the day. It ensures that nothing will interrupt their appointment with God. It is *first*.

If your students are anything like mine, they will argue that they are not "morning people." But the truth is, they will do *something* first every morning. Why not make it something that really counts?

Solitude will always seem like a waste of time to students if there is no purpose in it. Solitude without purpose breeds inconsistency and apathy. But solitude *with* purpose breeds discipline and intimacy. Jesus captured time for one reason: He wanted to experience intimacy with His Father. That should be our students' goal too.

How long should students meet with God, and what should they do during that time? We all have our ideas. The more important question is this: What will they walk away with after their time alone with God is done? What they do during their quiet time with God can vary. Using a devotional book (like the one we have produced as a companion to this book) is great. So is listening to a worship CD or finding a beautiful spot outside and sitting in silence. God loves variety. The important thing is that students don't wind up substituting routine for true intimacy and lose the wonder of their love relationship with their heavenly Father.

Time with God

There are three components that all students need to include in their time with God.

1. Read All about It

The first component is reading the Bible. God speaks to the core issues of our students' lives through the Scriptures. He roots out the anger behind the depression many teenagers experience. He uncovers the insecurity behind their self-destructive habits. He tells them how deeply they are loved and accepted. He draws them to Himself by explaining the price He paid to know them and to be known by them.

The Bible is much more than good literature. It is an active tool that can reveal the true condition of our students' minds and hearts. The writer of Hebrews illustrates this by saying, "For the word of God is living and active. Sharper than any double-edged sword, it penetrates even to dividing soul and spirit, joints and marrow; it judges the thoughts and attitudes of the heart."[4] If students are going to renew their minds and change their lives, the Word of God must be central to that process.

In their times with God, students can read as much or as little of the Bible as they want. As leaders we need to teach them to ask four key questions as they read:

✔ *What does this passage say?* They need to learn to summarize Scripture in their own words.

✔ *Why is this important?* They must understand why they need to know this fact or principle.

✔ *What should I do about it?* They need to learn how to specifically apply Scripture.

✔ *How can I remember this?* They need to cement what they learn by memorizing the verse, writing it on a card, or asking someone to hold them accountable for its contents.

Reading Scripture this way helps students understand God's value system—what's important to Him and why. It enables them to see things as God sees them, which in turn clarifies what He wants them to do and why He asks them to do it. In other words, through Bible reading students discover the *why* behind the *what*. For example, teenagers often hear adults say that they should honor their fathers and mothers. They hear that sex before marriage is wrong. "Why?" they ask. The Bible tells them *why* they should obey the *what*.

Students resist these and other commands because they don't see as God sees. They don't have His perspective. Stuart Hall, the coauthor of this book, illustrates the importance of perspective with the following true story:

As a parent I often find myself wanting to make my kids see things the way that I see them so they will do what I say. I remember going shopping for a Mother's Day present with my five-year-old son, Grant. I became so engrossed in trying to decide what to get for my wife that I didn't notice at first that Grant had wandered off. When I realized he was gone, I was frantic. I called out his name and searched under all the nearby racks of clothes.

Then something caught my eye. About three aisles away, I could see a man repeatedly bending over—up, down, up, down. It was a strange sight. I rushed to the area to see if my son was involved.

To both my delight and dismay the bowing man turned out to be a mannequin. Grant had a grip on its hands and was dancing merrily while he sang, "Gettin' Jiggy with It!"

Suddenly the mannequin tipped precariously on its stand. I grabbed it quickly to keep it from falling on my son. Then I began to explain why dancing with a mannequin was not the safest form of recreation. Grant's young mind could not understand, and he began to cry. He wanted to dance with the funny man! He couldn't see things the way I saw them; consequently, he didn't want to do what I said.

Our students have the biggest decisions of life ahead of them. Who will they marry? Where will they work? How will they fit into society? They also have big decisions to make right now. Should they obey their parents' curfew? Which friends will they hang out with this weekend? What will they do if someone offers them drugs at the party? What will happen if their date presses them for sex? If students can begin now to see as God sees, they will be much more inclined to do what He says in these decisive moments.

2. Praying Through

The second major component that must be included in our students' devotional time is prayer. Many teenagers say that they don't know how to pray or what to pray for. As leaders we can help by encouraging them to pray in concentric circles of concern—in other words, by beginning with those people and issues that are closest to their hearts and moving outward toward those things that are of less concern. We can also encourage them to:

✔ *pray through the passage they just read*—
"Lord, help me to be like the person I just read about."
"Lord, when I face a trial, remind me it is a test of my faith."

"Lord, help me to forgive _____ as You have for-given me."

✔ *pray through their day—*
"Lord, today I will be tempted to _____."
"Lord, today I am meeting with _____."
"Lord, today when he or she approaches me _____."

✔ *pray through their relationships—*
Family—"Lord, bless my mom today."
Friends—"Lord, help Karen to pass that test."
Acquaintances—"Lord, open Joshua's eyes to see you."

Prayer is simply talking with God. And teenagers certainly know how to talk! We need to help them learn to converse with their heavenly Father as naturally as they talk with their best friends. In fact, talking to God is *better* than talking to their best friends; He is the only one who loves them perfectly and always has their best interests at heart.

3. Write On!

The third major component of our students' time with God is journaling. A journal is simply a personal, written record of what God is teaching a particular student and what He is doing in his or her life. Its purpose is to record that student's spiritual pilgrimage. Students will write things in their journals—like how they're feeling at a certain point in time—that they normally would not express anywhere else or in any other way. This can be very healthy and freeing, especially during the tumultuous teenage years when emotions can be particularly difficult to process.

I have found that for students, journaling is probably better practiced as a weekly discipline rather than a daily one. But it is still important. Looking back is the only way for students to see how far they have come in their walk with God. I started keeping a journal when I was seventeen years old. Now whenever I get discouraged or think God has left me, a quick review of my journal is all I need to remind me that God is faithful and vitally active in my life. Students need to be able to do this in their lives too.

Memories

If your mom was anything like mine, you may have the distinct memory of having your mouth washed out with soap. I can still remember the inappropriate term that landed me in our avocado-green bathroom when I was fairly young. My bicycle fell in the driveway, and I said, "Get that ____ bicycle out of my way." At that exact moment, my mother stepped out onto the front porch. Funny how moms always seemed to appear at just the right times (or wrong times, depending on your perspective). I'm not sure what the theory is behind washing a child's mouth out with soap. But in my case, it was very effective.

That brings me to another aspect of a strong devotional life for students: Scripture memorization. Scripture memorization is the discipline of consistently and purposely washing our *minds* out with the "soap" of truth—God's Word. The difference? The Bible has no bad aftertaste!

Unlike Bible study, prayer, and journaling, Scripture memorization is something that students can (and probably should) do outside the confines of their scheduled quiet time. In fact, Scripture memorization and meditation on the Word of God are great ways for students to extend their devotional lives and continue to experience intimacy with God throughout the day.

Teenagers have the capacity to remember a lot of things. If something is important to them, they'll remember it: home phone numbers, work phone numbers, cell phone numbers, pager numbers, street addresses, web addresses, birthdays (including those of each of the Back Street Boys), anniversaries, important dates, what they wore last week to school, favorite menus and prices, measurements, song lyrics—the list could go on and on.

Can they memorize Scripture? Of course! The question is, Why should they? With more information at their fingertips than at any other time in history, with dozens of Bibles in a variety of translations always at their disposal, don't students have better things to do than fill their minds with more "stuff"?

"Besides," I've heard many students reason, "any problem I have can be answered when I get home or when I go to church on Sunday. There is no need for me to remember what God says, because most of the Bible doesn't relate to my everyday teenage life. What I need to remember is how to do calculus and trigonometry!"

For those students who have *not* grown up in church, making an effort to remember God's Word seems like one more "religious" thing to do. For those students who *have* grown up in church, Scripture memorization is one of those Sunday school competitions that never really connected with who they were and what they were dealing with at the time. They may have memorized a bunch of verses, but they have no idea what they mean or how they relate to their lives today.

So the question remains, why memorize God's Word? I'm getting to that!

I Think, Therefore...

Culture and society have systematically polluted the minds of our students with sin and lies since birth. Just think of your own progression of knowledge since childhood. When was the first time you heard a curse word? When was the first time you used one? When was the first time you pushed your way in front of others? When was the first time you purposely belittled another person? When was the first time you heard about sex? When was the first time you practiced what you heard?

The minds of our students are being polluted slowly but surely. With this progress comes the loss of innocence. Then gradually and without warning, the students begin to contribute to the pollution themselves.

Here's what Paul said in his letter to the church in Rome: "They [mankind] have become filled with every kind of wickedness, evil, greed, and depravity. They are full of envy, murder, strife, deceit and malice. They are gossips, slanderers, God-haters, insolent, arrogant and boastful; they invent ways of doing evil; they disobey their parents; they are senseless, faithless, heartless, ruthless."[5] Does that sound remotely like any students you know? It probably describes some of the sharpest teenagers in our ministries!

The fact is, our students' minds will either be their greatest strength or their greatest downfall. Students do what they do because of the way they think. To put it another way, a teenager's actions are simply the live movie version of the book of his or her thoughts. And believe me, your ministry and mine are full of teenagers who are not exactly excited about the "movie" playing in their "theater"! For example:

✔ The girl who always tends to be concerned about her clothes and makeup probably thinks her self-worth is based on how she looks.

✔ The guy who is physically aggressive with the girl he is dating probably thinks of that girl as an object and of sex as the basis for love.

✔ The girl who tends to overreact when she fails probably thinks that her significance is based on success.

✔ The guy who feels he has to work all the time probably thinks that significance is based on money or the acquisition of material things.

Each of these students is living out a live movie version of what they believe. Their mind is the script; their life is the running screenplay. Jesus alluded to this idea when He said, "What comes out of a man is what makes him 'unclean.' For from within, out of men's hearts, come evil thoughts, sexual immorality, theft, murder, adultery, greed, malice, deceit, lewdness, envy, slander, arrogance and folly. All these evils come from inside and make a man 'unclean.'"[6]

Is it any wonder that we have teenagers in our ministries who've made some type of commitment to God yet don't show any signs of it in the conduct of their lives? Our students *act* the way they do because of the way they *think*. The only way they will ever change the drama of their lives is by changing their script. Scripture memorization is a way for them to rewrite the script and change the movie—to take out the bad lines that produce an unexpected horror show and replace them with new, hopeful lines that guarantee a feel-good film with a happy ending.

Intentional Truth

To be effective, Scripture memorization must be a *consistent* discipline. Scriptures must be repeated over and over. We tend to connect the word *repetition* with *boring*. But repetition is a key to memorization. It is a key to learning. How did you learn to drive? To do math? To ride a bike or ski? To play the piano? To shoot a basketball? Repetition, of course!

Reading a verse is not memorizing it. And knowing a verse by heart is not even the issue. The point of this discipline is for students to get into the consistent habit of washing their minds out with the soap of God's Word. Out with the bad, in with the good. Think of a teenage girl and her fingernail polish. When she wants to put on new polish, she doesn't paint over the old, cracked polish that has been slowly peeling away. No, she first dabs an unbelievably stinky potion called polish remover on a cotton swab and removes the old polish. Then she applies the new polish to her nails. A week or two later, she repeats the same process over again. And a week later, she does it again. That's repetitious. That's continual. That's renewal!

Scripture memorization must also be *intentional* and *purposeful*. There is nothing worse for students than being asked to learn something that has no apparent value or application —like, say, trigonometry or Latin. Scripture memorization can be just as meaningless if students do it randomly. Asking students to memorize Leviticus 2:2 would be pointless; it would have no significance in their lives. All Scripture is inspired, but not all of it is applicable to teenagers! We need to point students in the direction of those verses that have particular application for their stage of life. We must help them identify the lies that have infiltrated their thinking and driven their behavior and encourage them to memorize those portions of God's truth that effectively replace those lies.

The Lie Detector

According to the apostle Paul, the lies our students believe are far from benign. These lies can become "strongholds"—

places where the enemy can "set up camp" and fortify his fight against them. Paul wrote: "For though we live in the world, we do not wage war as the world does. The weapons we fight with are not the weapons of the world. On the contrary, they have divine power to demolish strongholds. We demolish arguments and every pretension that sets itself up against the knowledge of God, and we take captive every thought to make it obedient to Christ."[7]

A stronghold takes students' minds off of God and His Word. It steals their focus. It causes them to feel controlled or mastered—and powerless to fight against it. How can students know if they have a stronghold in their lives? By asking themselves:

✔ What consumes most of my thoughts?

✔ What steals my focus away from the truth of God's Word?

✔ What controls my thinking?

✔ What is it that seems to be the master of my life?

Once students identify a stronghold or lie that has set up camp in their minds, they can choose the scripture or scriptures that combat that stronghold and memorize them. When the lie rises up, they can meet it and overcome it with God's truth. Being intentional like this in Scripture memorization makes the process useful and not just some religious exercise.

In my ministry I encourage students to "make truth visible"— to write their memory verses on index cards and keep them visible while they're at meals, watching TV, or talking on the phone. Students can attach their cards to their rearview mirror or the dash in their car. They can put their cards by their bed, on the ceiling above their bed, or on the bathroom mirror. I know students who have even written their verses on the bottom of the brim of their baseball hats! The important thing is for students to be reminded to think about how a particular scripture relates to them and how they can act on its truth. They can repeat the verse to someone, restate it in their own words, or bring it up during conversation with friends.

Ultimately, Scripture memorization will only work if it becomes a *priority* in our teenagers' lives. Halfhearted efforts to memorize a handful of Bible verses will never change minds or behaviors. But by taking the time and energy to memorize God's Word, to understand His Word, and to consistently wash their minds with His Word, our students can see their lives transformed. "How can a young man [or woman] keep his way pure?" the psalmist asks. "By living according to [God's] word. I seek you with all my heart; do not let me stray from your commands. I have hidden your word in my heart that I might not sin against you."[8]

Webster defines *memory* as "the power or process of reproducing or recalling what has been learned and retained through associative mechanisms." That process, Webster adds, is "evidenced by modification of structure or behavior." For students, the goal of memorizing Scripture is to renew their minds and in the process modify their behavior. Students can begin to react to life's struggles, tensions, and trials based on the recall of truth, not lies. A mind that is full of truth will result in a life that is exemplified by truth. When students begin to see as God sees, they will also begin to do as God says.

Be Strong and Take Heart

Remember Grant, the five-year-old son of Stuart Hall? Last October Grant began to experience some rectal bleeding. The problem, the doctors said, could be anything from a simple polyp to leukemia, and Grant would have to undergo surgery to make that determination.

Stuart remembers:

Needless to say, when cancer was mentioned, my heart sank to the ocean floor and fear ravished my mind and soul. I began to ask God for some kind of promise. I needed His perspective so I could act accordingly.

I remembered Psalm 31:24, a verse that I had taught our students not two weeks earlier. It said simply, "Take heart and be strong, all who hope in the LORD." I wrote the verse down for my wife and began to teach the verse to Grant, who was obviously afraid. When I picked him up from school for his pre-op tests, he looked up at me and said, "Daddy, I'm scared." I responded by reciting Psalm 31:24.

The day of the surgery, Grant was given a drug to make him drowsy. His speech became slurred, and he began batting at the air, convinced that cows were flying at him. It was actually quite comical.

Just before they rolled him back to surgery, Grant and I prayed together. When I finished praying, I noticed that he was whispering something under his breath. I leaned down and put my ear against his lips. He was repeating Psalm 31:24 over and over!

Grant was attacking fear with truth. At five years of age, he was already learning to see things as God sees them and to do as God says. Surely the teenagers in our youth ministries, by developing strong and vital devotional lives, can learn to do the same.

Checking In
Read Deuteronomy 6:1–11 and Psalm 119
Think about It

Journal your thoughts on this statement by Henri Nouwen:[9] "Solitude is the furnace for transformation." _____

_____

_____

_____

_____

How did God use solitude in the lives of each of the following men?

Abraham _____

_____

_____

_____

_____

Moses _____

_____

_____

_____

_____

Joshua _____

_____

_____

_____

Jonah _____

_____

_____

_____

David _____

_____

_____

_____

John the Baptist _____

_____

_____

_____

Jesus_____

_____

_____

_____

Do you consider God's Word an intimate part of your life? Why
or why not? _____

_____

_____

_____

_____

_____

In what areas of your life and ministry do you need to gain
God's perspective? _____

_____

_____

_____

If you were to title the movie of your life today, what would it
be and why? _____

_____

_____

_____

What do you do in your ministry to encourage students in the
spiritual disciplines? _____

_____

_____

_____

What are your students' greatest enemies when it comes to practicing spiritual disciplines? _____

_____

_____

_____

_____

Checkpoint #3
Moral Boundaries
Paving the Way for Intimacy

Principle

Purity paves the way to intimacy.

Critical Question

Are your students establishing and maintaining godly moral boundaries?

Key Passage

1 Thessalonians 4:3–8

And the way young people
talk about sex.
Sex is awesome, yeah,
but in the right
context.

—David Robinson
as quoted in *ESPN Magazine*

#3

Moral Boundaries

Paving the Way for Intimacy

Every opportunity I get I remind the students in my ministry that God created sex. I don't know how the idea occurred to Him. But I do know that a long time ago in a galaxy far, far away, there was no sex. Then one day God said to Himself, probably out loud, "I've got a great idea!"

OK, so maybe my imagination is a little irreverent. But the fact remains, sex is God's creation. It was and is God's idea. So it is safe to assume that He knows more about the subject than anyone—including Howard, Hugh, Dr. Ruth, and all of the assorted television and radio hosts who pollute the airways with their misinformation.

Sex can be unbelievably fulfilling (and fun). Or sex can leave a person feeling used and empty. Which do you suppose God intended? Sex is necessary for procreation, of course, but I think it is safe to assume that God wants our sexual experience to be fulfilling (and fun). So the next time you are making announcements in youth group, go ahead and praise God out loud for the wonderful gift of sex. Don't hold back. Say something like, "This is the day that the Lord has made. And I'm grateful for sex too! Isn't God good?"

My point? God desires for us to experience sex in a way that fully exploits the joy and fulfillment of this wonderful gift—and that's within a marriage relationship. He wants our sexual experience to be the best it can possibly be. God has created each of us with the potential to experience great sex. Yea, God!

Why Wait?

I'm not sure that's the message the church has communicated to our student culture. The notion that God is interested in the quality of their sex lives would cause most of our teenagers to do a double take. I imagine it might have caused you some slight discomfort in the past three minutes.

The message we've sent to our students is "wait until marriage." But "wait" is translated by many teenagers as just another big "no" to go along with all the other "no's" we have dumped on them. There is nothing enticing, stimulating, or motivating about "wait." For many of our teens, "wait" sounds like the desperate cry of an older generation looking to leverage their last bit of control over their kids' lives.

When we say "wait," the immediate outcry of our students is, "Why? Why wait?" We must answer that question! I'm convinced that we must shift the focus of our message to the *why* behind the *what*. There are many compelling reasons for reserving sex for marriage. Students need to know that sex in the right context is so wonderful, so special, that waiting is in their best interest.

The Intimate Connection

If I could drill one principle into the minds and hearts of students when it comes to sex, it would be this: *Purity paves the way to intimacy.* When we encourage kids to wait until marriage to experience sex, we are really asking them to remain pure. The question that must be answered then is, Why remain pure?

What's the advantage of purity? What do students gain by remaining pure that is better than what they give up?

The answer is simple: intimacy. Intimacy is the joy of knowing someone fully and being known by that person with no fear of rejection. Purity paves the way for intimacy. Impurity, on the other hand, erodes the capacity to experience intimacy—and consequently diminishes the satisfaction of sex.

If you have ever counseled people who've been sexually abused, you know that they always struggle to some degree with intimacy in marriage. Why? Because there is an inexorable link between purity and intimacy. Even unwanted sexual involvement affects an individual's capacity for intimacy. Men and women who've had affairs admit that even if they've been able to hold their marriages together, they can never achieve the intimacy they once had with their spouse. The impurity of their sinful actions has damaged their ability to be intimate. They can no longer be sure that they are knowing and being known without fear of rejection.

There is no escaping this principle. When people involve themselves sexually outside of marriage, they damage their capacity for intimacy.

This may be why Paul warned the Corinthians so strongly, "Flee from sexual immorality. All other sins a man commits are outside his body, but he who sins sexually sins against his own body."[1]

Our students need to know that when they sin sexually, they sin against themselves. They hurt themselves. They damage their potential for a satisfying sexual relationship with a marriage partner down the road. They rob their future spouse of intimacy as well.

I tell our young ladies: "You don't really want sex. What you want is intimacy. You want to meet a guy, fall in love, and know that you can trust that person completely. You want to share everything there is to know about you without fear of betrayal or rejection. You want to know that person fully and be fully known. What you are after is intimacy, not sex!"

Similarly, I challenge our young men: "Guys, I know what you want. You want to meet a girl you are physically attracted to, fall in love with her, and never lose that physical attraction. Your greatest fear is that you'll marry someone and then lose the attraction for her. You don't want to feel stuck. But the best way for you to ensure that you don't lose 'that loving feeling' is to set your sights on intimacy rather than sex. Great sex is the by-product of maximum intimacy."

In my years of ministry I have counseled dozens of attractive married couples who are no longer attracted to each other—couples whose sex lives are nonexistent. What happened? For all they knew about sex, they knew little to nothing about intimacy. And without intimacy, the sexual part of their relationship slowly died. We don't want that for our students' marriages. We need to teach them that purity now paves the way for intimacy later on.

More Than Physical

The reason satisfying sex and intimacy go together is because sex is not just physical; it is relational. Unfortunately, in our society sex is almost never talked about or portrayed in the context of long-term relationships. Movies, television, magazines, and popular music have ripped sex out of its relational context. Sex is almost always presented as something akin to a sporting event or activity—something (or someone) you *do*. Especially for our young men, sex is purely physical.

But God says sex is highly relational. That means that when students take sex out of its relational context, they will have problems. There will always be consequences. Sex will always be less than satisfying.

Take a look at how God described sex in the beginning:

So the LORD God caused the man to fall into a deep sleep; and while he was sleeping, he took one of the man's ribs and closed up the place with flesh. Then the LORD God made a woman from the rib he had taken out of the man, and he brought her to the man.

The man said, "This is now bone of my bones and flesh of my flesh; she shall be called 'woman,' for she was taken out of man." For this reason a man will leave his father and mother and be united to his wife, and they will become one flesh.[2]

When Adam and Eve had sexual relations, they didn't just "have sex." Something much more significant happened. They became one flesh. Through those intimate moments together, they were united.

The apostle Paul echoes this idea: "Do you not know that your bodies are members of Christ himself? Shall I then take the members of Christ and *unite* them with a prostitute? Never! Do you not know that he who unites himself with a prostitute is one with her in body? For it is said, 'The two will become one flesh.'"[3]

Our teenagers need to understand that simply "having sex" is not only not biblical, it is impossible! When two people come together sexually, they become one flesh. They are united. In other words, sex is not just physical. There is more to it than that.

Sex was designed by God as an expression of intimate oneness in body that matches a couple's commitment to oneness in purpose and direction in life. Each of our students is designed to become one with only one other person. That means that when they participate in sex outside of marriage, they forfeit the opportunity to become uniquely one physically with their future husband or wife. With every premarital sexual encounter, they decrease the significance of sex with their future partner. The oneness factor is damaged before it even exists.

If we don't tell our students about the ramifications of sex outside of marriage, who will? The question we must strive to keep in the forefront of their thinking is this: Are the temporary pleasures derived from premarital sex worth the long-term complications it will cause? My experience as a counselor and pastor has convinced me that the pain caused by sex before marriage far outweighs the pleasure. The pleasure is for a moment. The pain can last a lifetime.

God's Design

God knows all of this. That is why His will for our students is abstinence. Paul writes:

> It is God's will that you should be sanctified: that you should avoid sexual immorality; that each of you should learn to control his own body in a way that is holy and honorable, not in passionate lust like the heathen, who do not know God; and that in this matter no one should wrong his brother or take advantage of him. The Lord will punish men for all such sins, as we have already told you and warned you. For God did not call us to be impure, but to live a holy life. Therefore, he who rejects this instruction does not reject man but God, who gives you his Holy Spirit.[4]

To be sanctified means to become like Christ in character. That is God's design for our students. He wants them to become like His Son. God's will for them in relation to sex is that they wait.

Why? Because God is against sex? Because He wants our students to be miserable? On the contrary, God loves teenagers and wants the best for them. He wants their sexual experience to be the best it can possibly be. And He knows more about good sex than anyone does.

God is not against sex. He created it. God is not against teenagers. He created them. And God is not against their having sex. But He wants them to wait for marriage.

Sex is not for mature people. Sex is not for ready people. Sex is not for in-love people. Sex is for *married* people. Why? Because sex is not just physical; it is relational. It is to be reserved for the unique, committed, multifaceted relationship of marriage. Only between man and wife can sex be the wonderful and intimate experience that God always intended.

Relationships 101

For Men Only

During adolescence young men have a tendency to focus on the physical aspect of their relationship with women. Many of them do just enough of the relational part to "get their way." Consequently, many guys move through their teen years without learning anything about loving and honoring women. Instead, they learn to use them. Women become objects to be enjoyed rather than people to be cherished.

Since sex is relational, guys need to be encouraged to redirect their attention to developing great relational skills rather than pursuing sexual experience. Sexual experience now does not translate into sexual fulfillment later on. The very opposite is true.

The best thing a young man can do now to ensure a good relationship with his future wife is learn how to honor and respect the women God has already put in his life—namely, his mom and sister. As kinky as it sounds, he can prepare today for a great sex life later by learning how to love his mother and sister! Why? Because great sex is the by-product of a great relationship. And relational skills aren't magically embedded at the altar. They are learned over time.

We need to do everything in our power to help the young men in our student ministries shift their focus in relationships from the physical to the relational side of the equation. If they can learn to do this, they will have a much greater chance of keeping the physical and the relational in proper balance. The relationship skills they develop in the process will serve them well—with their future marriage partners and for the rest of their lives.

The Deal with Girls

Unlike the men in our groups, our young women tend to focus on the relational side of things even when there is only a fragile, temporary relationship in place. A teenage girl generally looks for assurances of commitment once things start to heat up physically. As the physical involvement increases, she wants more and more reassurance from her boyfriend that he really cares about her. That's why she suddenly feels inse-cure, used, and angry when the sexual relationship ends. It is also why she may quickly rebound into another unhealthy relationship.

Why this sudden sense of guilt and loss? Because sex is not just physical; it is relational. Women—even young women—know this deep in their hearts. As the number of her sexual encounters outside of marriage increases, a woman's security decreases. She begins to feel less and less valuable, less and less lovable.

As youth leaders we must communicate to our young women that God created them to be loved and cherished and honored. We must brand on their hearts that they should reserve the intimacy of sex for the men who commit to love, cherish, and honor them for a lifetime.

The Culture of Lies

Having removed intimacy from the equation, our culture is left with only the physical aspects of sex to talk about. And talk they do! Everywhere our students turn they are bom-barded with misinformation, half-truths, and flat-out lies. This endless proliferation of sexually oriented media messages marketed specifically to teenagers makes our job much more difficult. It is not enough for us to redefine the nature of sex for our students. We must also address the one-sided messages they are continually exposed to.

Here are six themes that are overtly and covertly woven into the culture, entertainment, and literature aimed at our teens:

1. Everybody is having sex.

To begin with, this is not a true statement. Secondly, it is not an argument for or against anything. It is simply a statement. The fact that everybody is doing something is not an argument in favor of that something. Because someone else does or does not do something is not a reason for our students to do it or not do it. We need to remind our teens that those students who are not having sex don't talk about it. There is nothing for them to talk about. There is a silent majority among their peers. As youth leaders we need to do everything we can to identify and honor that silent majority.

2. You can't live without sex.

Nobody says this directly, but it is certainly implied in much of the music of our culture. I know I have talked to many teenage girls through the years who admitted that they thought boys "had to have sex." They weren't sure where they heard this, but they assumed it was true. One young lady told me that she assumed her boyfriend was having sex with somebody somewhere since she wouldn't sleep with him. It may come as a shock to some of our students, but no one has ever died from *not* having sex. Yet thousands of people have died from AIDS and other sexually transmitted diseases (STDs) as a result of their sexual activity.

3. Sex is a natural part of a loving relationship.

If this is true, why can't those students who are so sexually active maintain long-term, loving relationships? I have counseled literally hundreds of students, and it is clear to me that sex is one of the primary reasons teenage relationships fall apart. Instead of sex making the relationship better, it drives a wedge between the two parties. If students want to know about real, fulfilling, long-term, loving relationships, direct them to an adult who has one.

4. Sex is a natural part of growing up.

The truth is sex keeps people from growing up. Our culture argues that the more sexual experiences teenagers have, the more grown-up they become. On the contrary, nature itself tells us it is not natural to have multiple sex partners. There are more than fifty types of venereal diseases that have been identified to date. Many are treatable but incurable. Some can even kill. Not only is it not natural to have multiple sex partners, it's not a healthy way to grow up.

5. Sex outside of marriage would cease to be a problem if teens would just wear condoms.

This widely held myth is the clearest indication that our society has divorced sex from intimacy and relationship. Everyone is warning students about the physical consequences of unprotected sex. Nobody is warning them about the emotional and relational consequences.

The message society sends is that the only problems related to sex before marriage are disease and pregnancy. If we stamp out unwanted pregnancy and STDs, we will have stamped out all the consequences of premarital sex. Right?

Wrong! Condoms do nothing to block the mental and emotional consequences of sex. A condom can't:

- ✔ erase a memory
- ✔ remove guilt
- ✔ restore a reputation
- ✔ repair self-esteem

6. Sex makes life better.

The truth is, sex outside of marriage doesn't make life better; it makes life more complicated. I will never forget my conversation with a woman who came to see me years ago. At that time Jenny was in her early thirties and had been divorced for eight years. She had only been a Christian for about six months. As soon as she sat down she said, "I have two questions. The first one is about the church, and the second one is personal."

I honestly can't remember her first question. But her second question is forever etched in my memory. She looked me right in the eye and said, "OK, about sex. Does the stuff in the Bible about sex being only for married people apply to somebody like me, or is it just for teenagers?"

At first I didn't know what to say. I knew what I believed, but I wasn't sure how to communicate it. Jenny noticed my hesitation. She went on to explain that since she had been married before, she wasn't sure if she was expected to remain celibate. From her perspective, not having sex seemed like an unreasonable expectation.

I stalled as long as I could. She deserved an answer. But I knew her faith was new and still quite immature. I was just about to launch into my "sex is for marriage only" sermonette when a question suddenly popped into my mind. To this day I believe God rescued both of us by turning my thoughts and words in a different direction.

I looked at Jenny and said, "Before I answer that question, let me ask you a question. Has sex outside of your marriage made your life better or just more complicated?"

She dropped her head and stared at the floor for a moment. Then she began to cry. Through sobs, she forced out her answer: "More complicated."

I waited for a minute before I said gently, "Jenny, that's why God has reserved sex for marriage."

Every day of our students' lives they are told that sex can have physical consequences. What this generation of teenagers never hears is that there are emotional, mental, and relational consequences as well. No one escapes. These consequences will follow them into one relationship after another and will ultimately impact their marriages. It is up to us to tell them the rest of the story!

"Fire in the fireplace is a wonderful thing," I tell my students. "But fire on the carpet can burn down your house. Sex is like fire. In the right context, it is awesome. But when it is outside the context it was designed for, sex can burn your life and your relationships to the ground. Don't play with fire!"

How Far Is Too Far?

If sex is out of the question, then what *can* our students do when it comes to their involvement with the opposite sex? How far can they go? If not all the way, how much of the way? Just how far is too far? Believe me, these questions are foremost on our teenagers' minds!

The Bible does not give a specific answer, but it does offer a general principle that students can follow: "Be very careful, then, how you live—not as unwise but as wise."[5] The question our students must learn to ask is, What is the wise thing for me to do? The writer of Proverbs tells us, "He who trusts in himself is a fool, but he who walks in wisdom is kept safe."[6] When it comes to keeping themselves pure, choosing the way of wisdom is the safest path for our teenagers to take.

Drawing the Line

Contrary to what they may think, however, wisdom is not hard to come by. Sometimes all it takes is just a little common sense. Here are four common-sense principles we must teach our students:

1. The further you go, the faster you go.

On the continuum that moves a couple from the starting point of "Hi, my name is _____" to the culminating point of sexual intercourse, there are many transition points. Students need to understand that every time their physical involvement with a person passes through one of those transition points and moves to a new level, their sense of fulfillment won't last as long as it did at the previous level of involvement. Desire accelerates. It never slows down.

2. The further you go, the further you want to go.

We can all remember the sensation we had the first time we held hands with that "special someone." At that moment holding hands was enough. It was almost too much! But before long the thrill began to wear off, and we wanted to take the relationship to the next level.

Teenagers need to understand that their sexual appetite is somewhat like their appetite for food. It is never fully and finally satisfied. When you feed an appetite, you increase both its capacity and its intensity. If you have ever tried to eat half of a dessert, you know what I mean. It is easier not to eat any at all! The more you eat, the more you want to eat.

When it comes to sex, students can draw a boundary line mentally, but that doesn't stem their desire physically. They will always want to go further. Short of intercourse, there is no "ultimate" satisfaction. Human bodies were designed to go "all the way." The only way students can keep their sexual appetites in check is not to feed them!

3. The further you go, the harder it is to go back.

A teenager I'll call Donna came to my wife during a summer youth camp with tears streaming down her face. Unfolding her story between sobs, she explained that her father had forbidden her to see a particular guy. She had disobeyed, however, and she and the boy had begun dating behind her father's back. Before long they had gotten sexually involved. The relationship had been going on now for several months, and Donna was riddled with guilt.

After talking with my wife, Donna resolved to break off her relationship. She was a different girl from July to December. God began to move in her life in ways that were obvious to us and to her peers, and she became a leader in our ministry. Her old boyfriend kept calling, but she resisted his advances and pleas for a second chance.

After Christmas Donna decided to see the boy just once—"out of kindness," she said. But instead of starting over, the two picked up where they left off, and Donna got pregnant. My wife took Donna to the doctor to confirm the pregnancy. I had the heartbreaking task of telling her mom and dad. Because Donna chose to ignore the principle of "the further you go, the harder it is to go back," her life has been changed forever.

Our students need to know that God did not design them to go back. He designed them to move forward sexually. Consequently, it is almost impossible to permanently retreat to safety once certain lines have been crossed.

4. *Where you draw the line determines:*

> ✔ **the arena of your temptation**

If a young man decides that the line for him is kissing, then he has determined what he will be tempted to do next—namely, whatever he perceives the next step to be after kissing.

If he decides that oral sex is OK, then he has determined the arena of his next temptation as well. We must tell our students that every conviction has a corresponding temptation. When they set their standards, they also determine their next temptation.

✔ the intensity of the temptation

Temptation increases with increased passion, and passion increases as a couple moves closer and closer to intercourse. Every couple is going to be tempted. As we provide guidance to our teenagers we need to ask them, "Assuming you will be tempted to go further than you choose, how intense do you want that temptation to be?" We must remind them that where they draw the line determines the intensity of the temptation. They are actually choosing the level of pressure they will feel in their dating relationships.

✔ the consequences of giving in to temptation

If a couple has decided that holding hands is far enough, and one night after a romantic date at Steak and Shake they get carried away and actually kiss, what are the consequences? A touch of guilt, perhaps. Worst-case scenario, somebody gets strep throat. But if a couple has drawn the line at the edge of intercourse…you get the picture.

We need to explain to our students that they are determining their own destiny by choosing where they draw the line. From time to time passions will run high, and even the strongest Christian may temporarily allow his or her standards to slip. Where students have drawn the line will determine the nature of the consequences once that line has been crossed.

What's Your Story?

The whole "How far is too far?" question is very confusing for the students in our ministries. It doesn't help that they are immersed in a culture that thinks the question is bogus to begin with. The issue for most teenagers is, How far *can* I go? not, How far *should* I go?

When I was moving through the maze of adolescence, a different question brought this whole issue into focus for me: How far would I want my future wife to go with the person she dated right before meeting me? I must admit I really hated that question. Sometimes determining how far I should go was difficult, but I always knew exactly how far the person I would one day marry should go: *not very far*.

Unfortunately many of our students are already living with the guilt and regret of having gotten too involved sexually. Those students need to be reassured of God's grace and forgiveness. But they also need to be challenged to pursue purity along with the rest of the kids.

Whenever I talk to students about sex I always remind them that regardless of what they've done in the past, they can begin again. The fact that they went "too far" is no reason to give up the fight and give in to temptation. I remind them that someday they are likely to meet the person they want to spend the rest of their life with. When they do, they will have one of three stories to tell:

Story One

"When I was a teenager I messed up sexually. I got carried away with the person I was dating. I figured that since I did it once, it really didn't matter if I did it again. So I slept with several other people along the way to meeting you."

Story Two

"When I was a teenager I messed up sexually. But when I was ____ years old, after hearing my youth leader teach on moral boundaries, I decided that God knew what He was talking about. Sex was created for marriage. I decided that from that point on I would wait. I set new standards and have stuck with them. Since that day I have saved myself for you."

Story Three

"When I was a teenager I realized that God knows more about sex than anyone. Since He created sex for marriage, I decided to wait. I have saved myself for you."

After telling the three possible stories, I ask the kids, "Which story do you want to tell? Which story would you want to hear from the person you choose to marry?" Our students need to answer these questions and make their decisions accordingly.

Check Your Destination

If some of your students were waiting on a street corner to catch a bus, they wouldn't necessarily get on the first bus that pulled up to the stop. They would look at the sign to see where that bus was going. Yet every day teenagers are being invited to board the bus of sexual immorality that is carrying thousands of their peers to lives of misery, guilt, and pain. Before they board, they need to check the destination! It is up to us to tell our students both the truth about God's wonderful creation of sex and the lies our culture continues to spew at them to cloud their vision.

You and I need to encourage the teenagers in our ministries to establish godly moral boundaries. We need to help them map out plans for remaining pure until marriage. Purity, after all, paves the way to intimacy. And intimacy—between one man and one woman committed in marriage—provides the one perfect context for a lifetime of satisfying sexual experience.

Checking In
Read 1 Corinthians 6:18 and 1 Thessalonians 4:3–8
Think about It

Revisit the six themes on pages 89–92 and write down specific television shows, movies, and songs that currently promote these lies to your students. _____

_____

_____

_____

_____

_____

_____

_____

What is the message that you've been giving your students about sex? When you tell them to wait, do you give them the *why* behind the *what*? _____

_____

_____

_____

According to 1 Corinthians 6:18, how should your students deal with sexual immorality? _____

_____

_____

_____

What does Paul mean by "sanctified" in 1 Thessalonians 4:3?

_____

_____

_____

What three things does Paul say are God's will for your students in sanctification? What are you doing in your ministry to encourage them in these three things? _____

_____

_____

_____

_____

What do you think Paul means when he says "the Lord will punish men for all such sins"?_____

_____

_____

_____

_____

Checkpoint #4
Healthy Friendships
Choosing Friends for Life

Principle

Your friendships determine the direction and quality of your life.

Critical Question

Are your students establishing healthy friendships and avoiding unhealthy ones?

Key Passage

Proverbs 13:20

If you sleep with dogs,
you are going to get fleas.

—SOUTHERN PROVERB

#4

Healthy Friendships
Choosing Friends for Life

We all have had friends who've made a significant impact on our lives. Perhaps you came to faith in Christ because of a friend. Or maybe a friend led you into some trouble that you now regret. For good or for bad, our friends have played a major role in determining the quality and direction of our lives.

The same is true for the students in our youth ministries today—and more so. Back in the 1960s, a Gallup poll showed that the top three influences in a teenager's life were:

- ✔ parents
- ✔ teachers
- ✔ spiritual leaders

But the playing field has shifted dramatically. According to a more recent survey, the top three influences in a teenager's life today are:

✔ friends
✔ media—music, television, movies, etc.
✔ parents

(Not to discourage you, but spiritual leaders dropped to number seventeen on the list. Essentially, we don't exist!)

Our response to this stunning shift in influence should be obvious. As youth leaders we must ensure that our students understand the influence their friends have in their lives. As parents we must accept our teenagers for the unique creations that they are and not let their friends "out-accept" us. Together we must do everything we can to make sure that the peers who influence our students are leading them in God's direction. Our teenagers need to know that their friendships will determine the direction and quality of their lives.

The Power of Influence

I will never forget a couple of friends I had in the third grade. Bradley, Gary, and I were like "The Three Amigos." We were always getting into trouble, always causing chaos, and always inventing some new way to become infamous. One day Bradley and Gary decided to seal their bond with me by making me take the Sissy Test. Remember the Sissy Test? Someone would take the eraser end of a pencil and rub it on the back of your hand as fast as they could until your hand bled or you screamed. If you screamed, you were a sissy and no longer a friend. Well, I screamed *and* bled. And I screamed again when I got home and my dad found out what I had done.

Can you believe it? I became a sissy, gained a scar, lost my best buddies, and got a spanking—all because of the powerful influence of friends. Before you laugh too hard, think back. Chances are you did some pretty ridiculous things at the urging of friends too!

The question we must ask ourselves is this: Are the students in our youth ministries establishing healthy friendships and avoiding unhealthy ones? The answer will play a major role in how our teenagers conduct themselves throughout middle school and high school. It will determine where they end up in their spiritual journey. Why? Because the friendships our students choose will determine both the direction and the quality of their lives.

Some may be tempted to argue with this principle. "Isn't that a little extreme?" they might ask. "Can a teenager's friends really have so much influence?" Absolutely. Here are a few observations that substantiate this claim:

1. Friends often have a greater influence on a teenager than the teenager's own convictions.

Eventually all students are faced with a choice between their friends and their convictions. When I ask teenagers to raise their hands if they have ever temporarily abandoned a conviction at the urging of a friend, every hand in the room goes up. Most of our students don't have to reach back too far to remember an occasion when they were forced to choose between the acceptance of their friends and their deeply held beliefs.

This dynamic explains why so many decisions made for

Christ at a weekend retreat or summer camp are abandoned within hours of the church bus pulling back into the parking lot. Let's say Bobby decides to give his life to Jesus at the end of an exciting retreat. He leaves the commitment service determined to do the right thing, to make some real changes. The partying is going to stop. He is going to break it off with his girlfriend. No more lying to his parents. But what happens? Bobby goes back to an environment where the need for acceptance from his friends outweighs his convictions. Gradually he slips back into the life that he renounced at camp. Why? Because Bobby's friends have a greater influence on him than his convictions.

2. Friends often have a greater influence on a teenager than the teenager's parents do.

This is baffling. It is especially baffling when we consider the sacrifices the average parents make for their children. One would think that out of sheer gratitude students would continue to give Mom and Dad the lion's share of their devotion and respect. But that wasn't the case when we were teenagers. And it certainly is not the case now.

On paper it doesn't make sense that fourteen-year-olds would put more stock in the advice of other fourteen-year-olds than in the advice of the grown men and women who would die for them at a moment's notice. But they do. That's the power of friendship.

With the tragic breakdown of family structures in our society, friends are given even greater leverage in the lives of teenagers today. If students don't feel unconditional acceptance at home, they will find it among friends. This explains in part the sudden rise in the formation of gangs. What was once considered an inner-city problem now haunts small towns in Middle America. For many teenagers, both male and female, gangs have replaced the family unit as the primary environment of acceptance. In many cases, a teenager's peers have taken the reins of influence away from Mom and Dad.

3. A teenager's friends often have greater influence over him or her than God does.

Ask your students if friends have ever influenced them to do something they knew was contrary to God's will for their lives. Sure they have. Haven't we all!

In other words, some sixteen-year-old whom Bobby has known for all of four months is able to persuade him to temporarily turn his back on the God of the universe in order to do something he won't even remember a year from now. That's a lot of power. Think about it—a sixteen-year-old who has the power to out-influence God!

Now do you see why I say that our students' friendships will determine the direction and quality of their lives? Nobody can compete with friends. Not even God.

This principle is supported by more than mere observation. In Proverbs 13:20, Solomon, the wisest person who ever lived, said, "He who walks with the wise grows wise, but a companion of fools suffers harm." Both a promise and a warning are included in this verse. The promise is that if your students walk with wise friends, they in turn will grow wise. The warning is that students who associate themselves with foolish friends will suffer harm. Let's take a closer look at each side of this equation.

The Promise

If students spend the majority of their time with wise people, they will become wise. In other words, the "wise" will rub off on them. But what does that mean? What does it mean to be wise? And is it really that important? If our students don't understand the benefits of being wise, this verse doesn't provide much leverage. But if somehow we are able to create a thirst in their hearts for wisdom, then this verse has the potential to redirect their thinking about friends.

One of the most productive teaching series I've ever done with my students was built around the three types of people mentioned in the book of Proverbs: the wise, the fools, and the scoffers. Using a concordance, I looked up every verse in Proverbs that mentions these characters. Then I made a list of the terms and phrases Solomon uses to describe each one. I spent several weeks talking to our students about the benefits and blessings associated with wisdom. I showed them why it is better to be wise than to be a fool or a scoffer. For many of the teenagers in our group, that study created a real hunger for wisdom. And once that hunger kicked in, the significance of Proverbs 13:20 began to take hold in their lives.

Over the long haul, the pursuit of wisdom will do more to motivate our students to rethink their friendships than anything else they can do. Create a hunger in their hearts for wisdom, and we will have the tool we need to help them establish healthy relationships and avoid unhealthy ones.

Hard to Spot

A wise person is someone who knows the difference between right and wrong and chooses to do what's right—even when it's hard. Unwise teenagers are pretty easy to spot. Wise ones are generally harder to find.

In fact, students are often quick to object to this principle about healthy friendships because they think they don't know any "wise" peers. If wisdom is the primary criteria for friendship, they feel as if they are facing the prospect of no friends at all!

Wise friends are somewhat like owls. They are out there. They're just hard to spot. Why? For one thing, owls are quiet. They are still. They tend to blend in with the environment without making a scene. The few times I have seen owls in their natural habitat, someone has had to point them out to me. When they do make noise, the sound is unmistakable. But more times than not, finding an owl requires patient observation and a process of elimination. (*No, that's not an owl. Not that one either. That's not it. Not in that tree, or that one....*)

Students need to understand that finding a wise friend can be a similar process. He or she may be difficult to spot at first. But by observing from a safe distance and noting the students who tend to make poor choices and suffer the consequences, they will be able to narrow the choices for a healthy friendship.

Several years ago a particular beer commercial sported the

motto, "Good times are made for good friends...it doesn't get any better than this." A scene slowly evolved of a group of friends sitting around a lakeside campfire, eating fresh fish and drinking beer. The implication was that beer created good times that could only be experienced with good friends.

Our students need to be reminded that good friends are wise friends. Good friends know the difference between right and wrong. Good friends make good decisions. And it will always be easier for teenagers to do the right thing when they are with the right people.

The Warning

Proverbs 13:20 also contains a warning—one that most of our students will quickly identify with: "A companion of fools will suffer harm." In other words, if students spend the majority of their time with foolish friends, they will experience painful consequences.

A fool is someone who knows the difference between right and wrong but chooses to do what is wrong. Fools simply don't care about doing right. They are not ignorant—just uninterested. Pointing out the consequences of an action does not stop foolish people; they just do what they want to do when they want to do it. They feel that they are invincible. When it comes to using deception to serve their purposes, they don't hesitate. In fact, they are convinced they're superior to others when they successfully pull the wool over someone's eyes.

Hanging around with fools doesn't mean that our students will become fools. It's worse than that. Something bad will eventually happen to them. When teenagers associate with foolish friends, they unintentionally put themselves in harm's way. They make themselves a target. The verse doesn't say that harm *might* happen. It clearly states that the friend of fools *will* suffer harm.

One of the recurring arguments teenagers use with their parents and youth leaders goes like this: "But I don't do what they do. I just want to be where they are." Or, "I don't drink; I just go to the parties."

Our students need to understand: It is not always *what they do* that causes them to get hurt. It is *whom they are with*. It is the companion of fools—not necessarily the fools themselves—who will suffer harm.

A Painful Reminder

For all of us who knew Josh Ming, Saturday, April 9, 1994, will always stand as a cruel reminder of the importance of healthy friendships. Josh was driving his cousin and two female passengers to a house in Shreveport, Louisiana, when four teenagers standing in the street began firing on the car. Josh was shot in the back of the head and killed in what police described as a "hail of gunfire." An estimated fifty-plus bullets hit the car.

The four teenagers arrested in the fatal shooting were known members of a gang of middle- and upper-class teens called "The Fighting Irish." Josh's cousin was suspected of being involved in gang activity, as were the two girls in the car.

Josh was just giving his cousin a ride.

Josh was not a fool. He had given his life to Christ, and the change had been evident. Josh participated regularly at our weekly outreach event. He helped teach the children's choir at the church with his girlfriend, Jennifer. He was a member of the Airline High School football team. His grades were improving. Life was good.

On this one night, however, he was the *companion of fools*, and he suffered harm.

Again, the focus of this warning is not on *what* our students do. The focus is on *whom* they are with.

Under the Influence

I think most students recognize that their friends have an impact on their lives. But few of them understand *why* they are so susceptible to the influence of friends. It is difficult for any of us to break a pattern of behavior if we don't know what's driving us in that direction to begin with. Students operate under the assumption that they have freely chosen their friends. Nothing could be further from the truth.

Gravitational Pull

If some teenagers in your ministry approached you and asked how they should choose a friend, what would you say? Would you tell them to interview candidates? Would you advise them to walk around with a list of desired characteristics, match them against the people they know, and yell "Bingo!" when they find someone who meets all the criteria? Think about it. What does it mean to "choose a friend"?

The truth is our students don't really choose their friends. If they did, I probably wouldn't need to write this chapter. If our teenagers were carefully choosing their friends, their networks of relationships would look much different than they do.

From time to time I ask my students to make of list of the top five qualities they want in a friend. Then I ask them to list the top five qualities they want in the people they date. Over and over these students admit that their current friendships and dating relationships fall short of what they are really hoping for. Why? Because they didn't choose these friends. They merely gravitated toward acceptance. They hooked up with the people who were most accepting of them.

Teenagers are *acceptance magnets*. Watch some students walk into a party and you will witness this principle in action. Those students will naturally begin to communicate and interact with other peers who make them feel accepted. They will steer clear of the student or group of students that they sense dislikes or rejects them.

Teenagers don't really choose their friends. *Their friends choose them.*

Acceptance is one of the strongest drives in life. Everybody wants to be liked, right? Students make decisions about their appearance and conduct based primarily on how it will affect their standing with those to whom they look for acceptance. They try to wring acceptance out of just about every environment in which they live, work, and play.

That is why some of our students can act so spiritual at youth group and live like the devil on the weekends. They want to fit in, and they are willing to adapt themselves to different environments in order to gain the acceptance they crave. Bottom line, their choice of friends has more to do with their desire to be accepted than a list of characteristics they've drawn up. They don't *choose* their friends. They gravitate toward acceptance.

So Prove It

When I challenge students with this concept, they are usually quick to take offense. On the surface it sounds like I am making them out to be extremely insecure. So I ask them the following questions:

✔ **Have you ever lied to keep from looking bad?**

Sure they have. Why? Because they would rather lie than face the rejection of friends. Acceptance is too important. As a follow-up question I ask, "How many of you believe it is wrong to lie?" They all raise their hands. They all have been willing to abandon a conviction for the sake of acceptance.

✔ **Have you ever stolen something you didn't need because the friend you were with stole something?**

Sheepishly, a few hands always go up. Mostly guys. Then I ask, "How many of you believe stealing is wrong?" All the hands go up. Once again, the incredible power of acceptance has won out over conviction! To make the kids squirm a little more I ask, "If you were making a list of characteristics you want in a friend, how many of you would include 'thief'?" No hands.

When students think that their acceptance is at stake, there is almost nothing they won't do to secure it. I know a young lady who was suspended for several days during her sophomore year in high school for shoplifting alcohol from a grocery store. Get this: She did the deed while she was on a school field trip (obviously not the sharpest tool in the shed). Later she admitted she didn't even drink. She was stealing the booze for her friends.

✔ How many of you have friends who have self-destructive habits that you have never said anything about?

When hands start to rise, I ask, "Why? If you are really their friend, why don't you confront them?" Eventually someone in the group will admit the truth: They don't want to appear nosy or risk making their friend angry. In other words, they are not willing to risk losing a friendship even if it means possibly saving the friend's life. Acceptance by a friend is more important than the friend!

As youth leaders we need to help our students understand that they have surrounded themselves with friends whose acceptance is more important to them than almost anything else—more important than their convictions, more important than their integrity, even more important than the welfare of the friends themselves! They didn't choose these people as friends. They simply found an environment of acceptance.

The Other Side

Acceptance is only one side of the coin, however. Our students not only gravitate toward acceptance; they flee rejection. Nothing hurts like being rejected by peers. Students will go to extreme measures to avoid it.

Listen as Stuart Hall recounts this story of rejection from his childhood:

> Because of my family's financial status when I was growing up, I never had the coolest name-brand clothes. One year my parents bought me two pair of Sears Tuffskin jeans for school, a brown pair and a blue pair. All the cool kids had Levis with the silver or red tabs. I had two pair of Tuffskins that had to last all year! When my jeans started wearing out and getting holes in them, my mom, who was big into cross-stitching, made a huge Indian head on the leg of my brown jeans and an American flag on the rear end of my blue jeans. I can still hear kids pledging allegiance to my rear end and calling me "Tonto." I vowed that I would never have to face that kind of rejection again.

Like Stuart, most teenagers have been laughed at or put down enough to know that they want to avoid rejection at any cost. Eric Harris, one of the two young gunmen in the 1999 Columbine High School tragedy, wrote in his academic day planner, "The lonely man strikes with absolute rage." Harris and his accomplice, Dylan Klebold, both wrote privately of not being accepted, of being rejected, of not fitting in. Investigators who analyzed their writings concluded, "They plotted against all those persons who found them offensive— jocks, girls who said no, other outcasts, or anybody they thought did not accept them."[1]

Clearly rejection and acceptance are powerful forces in the lives of teenagers. This explains why some students in our youth groups can't seem to break away from destructive relationships. To leave the relationship means abandoning an environment of acceptance. That's hard to do—especially when they feel like they have no other safe harbors. Simply pointing out to students the consequences of destructive relationships is not enough to get them to change. Acceptance covers a multitude of consequences!

The Missing Link

Perhaps I'm making acceptance sound like a bad thing. It's not. There is nothing wrong with teenagers wanting to be accepted. But acceptance by the wrong people can be detrimental to their lives. Why? Because *acceptance paves the way to influence*.

This is a principle that every student pastor, youth worker, and parent must keep in sight at all times. Acceptance and influence are inexorably linked. Think about it: Students resist the influence of those they feel don't accept them. When they feel accepted, however, they drop their guard.

What this means is that our homes and youth groups must be the most accepting environments our students experience. We must out-accept the competition. That is the only way we will develop sustained influence with our teenagers. They won't embrace our message until they are assured of our love and acceptance.

And what is our message? *Students must choose what they want out of life before they allow someone to choose them for a friend.* Setting a course for life will help students steer clear of friends who will not help them reach their goals and potential. To do otherwise would be like shooting a hole in the side of a wall and then painting a bull's-eye around that hole. Instead of setting a goal and aiming for it, students would find themselves at a destination and simply settle for it. They'd relinquish the power to determine the direction and quality of their lives to others. Their lives would be guided by whom they "run with" rather than what they could become and accomplish. Peers would replace potential.

I have never seen students make significant, long-lasting changes in their lives without making some changes in the area of friendships. Like you, I have seen students make all sorts of commitments. But unless they are willing to tackle this sensitive area, their progress will be short-lived. It is almost impossible for students to change their focus and direction in life without making adjustments in the friends who surround them.

For Those Who Choose to Choose

Acceptance *is* an important part of a friendship. But it is only one part. After all, those students who end up in detention centers or drug rehabilitation units have friends who accept them. Oftentimes these are the friends who got them involved in trouble to begin with. Acceptance is important, but it isn't enough.

God wants our students to have real friends, not just people who accept them. So what should our students be looking for in the people they allow into their inner circle? What does a *true* friend look like?

True Friends

A true friend is someone who will *love* you and not just *accept* you. You can accept people without really loving them. But if you truly love them, you will certainly accept them. A true friend is one who accepts you just the way you are—but who loves you too much to leave you that way.

In a friendship where acceptance is the only glue holding people together, there will be little confrontation. No one will be willing to risk upsetting the other person. No one will say the things that need to be said.

But true friends are more committed to their friend than to the friendship—more concerned about what's best for their friend than about being accepted by that person. I think of the tragic example of the late comedian Chris Farley. I can't count the number of times I heard people on TV who considered themselves to be Chris's best friends bemoan his death. Yet they admitted that they never confronted him about his alcohol and drug abuse. They chose to ignore these obvious issues for the sake of gaining and keeping Chris's acceptance. After all, he was famous. They were so enamored with what they gained from the relationship that they ignored what was best for Chris. Apparently they were more committed to the friendship than to the friend.

Counterfeit Friends

People who accept our teenagers but don't have their best interests in mind are really counterfeit friends. Just as there is counterfeit money, there are counterfeit friends. Our students need to know how to spot a counterfeit. For the most part counterfeit friends look like a friend, act like a friend, and feel like a friend. But they aren't the genuine item.

A counterfeit friend is far worse than an enemy. Our students' enemies may hurt them temporarily, but a counterfeit friend can ruin their lives. With an enemy, their guard is up. But when they are with people they consider friends, they are wide open to their influence. Their greatest regrets will generally involve people they thought were their friends.

Two things make counterfeit friends particularly dangerous. The first is this: *A counterfeit reduces the incentive to seek out the real thing.* If you had an endless supply of counterfeit money that was accepted everywhere as the real thing, how motivated would you be to work? Why labor for the real thing when the counterfeit works just as well? Similarly, if a counterfeit friend provides acceptance, why work at developing new and genuine relationships?

Students who have surrounded themselves with counterfeit friends don't feel the need to add anybody else to their inner circle. As their youth pastors, we may see their need for more wholesome relationships, but they won't. Many times, it is not until the counterfeit is removed that teenagers find the incentive to begin looking for the real thing.

Secondly, *a counterfeit is hard to leave behind.* Think how difficult it would be to toss a bag full of counterfeit hundred dollar bills—bills that would be readily accepted all around town—into a fire. It is difficult to leave a counterfeit behind. It is difficult for our students to end a relationship with a counterfeit friend. I tell our students all the time, "The most difficult thing you will do as a teenager is walk away from relationships with people you really care about." It is difficult, but sometimes it is necessary.

Spotting a Counterfeit

As students evaluate the genuineness of their friendships, they need to be sensitive to three factors:

1. The Direction of the Relationship

Relationships don't stand still; they are always moving in one direction or another. Students have a tendency to evaluate a friendship based on where it is at a particular point in time. They need to be aware of the direction of the relationship as well as what is happening at any given moment.

Genuine friendships move in a positive, mutually beneficial direction. A counterfeit friend will move the relationship the other way. Students must ask themselves, "If this relationship continues to move in the current direction, where will it eventually end up?" And secondly, "Is that where I want to be?"

2. Self-Destructive Behavior

Counterfeit friends will usually exhibit some form of self-destructive behavior. Perhaps they will seem incapable of making wise choices. They may tend to get in the same trouble over and over. Most likely they will scorn the authority figures in their lives.

The reason self-destructive behavior is important for students to look out for is that if their friends won't watch out for themselves, they certainly won't be looking out for anyone else. If someone doesn't take good care of his or her car, I would think twice before I loan that person mine!

3. A Lack of Solid Convictions

A person who lacks convictions will have a difficult time being a true friend. Students should listen for statements such as:

✔ **"You have to do what you feel is right for you."**

✔ **"Everybody has to decide for themselves."**

✔ **"No one can tell other people what is right for them."**

These are the mantras of those who have no solid convictions—who drift along with the emotion of the moment. When our students must stand up for what is right in the sight of God (but unpopular), these friends won't stand be standing with them.

Circles of Friendship

When we talk about true versus counterfeit friends, we don't want our students to get the idea that we don't care about their friends who are less than perfect. Nor do we want them to think that we don't want them to have relationships with peers who need Christ. We simply want them to be wise and put all of their relationships in proper perspective. One of the best ways I've found to do this is to introduce them to the idea of concentric circles of friendship, as the following diagram illustrates:

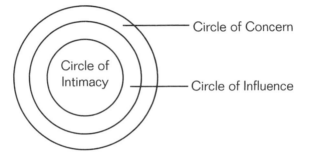

The concentric circles model helps students see that the issue is not whether or not their friends are "good people." It is whether or not their friendships are healthy and going in the right direction.

We need to explain to our students that all of their friends fall into one of three categories. The outer circle represents those friends they are concerned about. These may be their non-Christian friends or Christian friends who are going through a tough time—anyone they consider a friend and for whom they feel a sense of concern. These are peers they hope to influence.

The second circle, the circle of influence, represents the friends they allow to have influence in their lives. There's no mystery here. Students know who their positive and negative influences are.

The third circle, the circle of intimacy, is reserved for one person: the man or woman they will someday meet, fall in love with, and marry. Including this circle gives us the opportunity to remind our students that whom they date matters. It is easy for teenagers to allow their feelings of mercy and concern to evolve into romantic interest. Therefore they need to be sure they choose the people they date from their circle of influence, not their circle of concern.

Once our students understand this concept, the issue then becomes what to do with those friends who are in the second circle but who are negative influences. These counterfeit friendships must be addressed. What that actually means will depend upon the circumstances surrounding each friendship. Students don't necessarily have to abandon these friends, but they must at least move them further out into their circle of concern. Perhaps one day these friends will be able to move into a place of positive influence. But until the people change, the friendships must change.

What Are the Options?

When it comes to moving counterfeit friends out of their circle of influence, students have three options. They can do nothing; essentially, they can decide not to decide. But time is their enemy, not their ally, in counterfeit friendships. The longer they wait, the harder it will be to make a change. And in the meantime they leave their lives open to their friends' negative influence.

A second option is to take a step back. By this I mean students can adjust the amount of time they spend with a particular friend. They can also make an effort to take more control of the relationship—to conduct the friendship on their terms rather than their friend's terms. For example:

- ✔ They can invite the friend to their home rather than spending time at their friend's house.

- ✔ They can begin choosing the movies, music, and videos they share.

- ✔ They can be the driver instead of the passenger when they go places.

- ✔ They can choose where to hang out.

In this option, our students lead the relationship; they set the pace. If the friend won't go along, however, they may have to consider the third option: stepping away from the relationship altogether. Many students object to this idea, saying, "What's going to happen to my friend if I just walk away?" But the real issue is what is going to happen to our students if they *don't*.

Admittedly, making adjustments in counterfeit friendships is a painful process. One of the most difficult things our teenagers will be called upon to do is to walk away from relationships with people they really care about. It is difficult, but it must be done. After all, their friends—especially those within their circle of influence—will determine the direction and quality of their lives.

The Big Relationship

What our teenagers need are true friendships built on love and acceptance. They need friends who demonstrate a healthy respect for their convictions. For our students who are Christians, this translates into friends who respect and encourage their relationship with God.

I constantly quiz my students about this aspect of their friendships. I ask, "Do your friends encourage or hinder your walk with Christ?" I remind them that they should never sacrifice their relationship with God for a relationship with another person. God must take priority. That means they must guard against friendships that slowly chip away at their convictions. True friends, Christian or not, will always encourage their deeply held beliefs.

Ultimately, friendships will determine the direction and quality of all of our lives. You and I already know this from personal experience. Now let's do everything we can to ingrain this simple but life-changing principle in the minds and hearts of all the students we can reach.

Checking In
Read Proverbs 13:20; 14:8; and 13:10
Think about It

According to Proverbs 13:20, what is the result of having a relationship with a wise person? What is the result of having a relationship with a fool? _____

_____

_____

_____

_____

_____

_____

_____

Have you ever suffered harm because of a friend? What happened and why? _____

_____

_____

_____

_____

_____

_____

According to Proverbs 14:8, what is "the wisdom of the pru-
dent"? What is "the folly of fools"?_____

_____

_____

_____

_____

_____

_____

What is the root cause of the quarrels that follow a fool according to Proverbs 13:10?_____

_____

_____

_____

Do you think the identity of the writer of Proverbs gives validity to these principles about relationships? _____

_____

_____

_____

_____

_____

Think of the students in your youth group. Can you tell which ones have true friends surrounding them? Which ones are most susceptible to the influence of counterfeit friends?

_____

_____

_____

_____

_____

_____

_____

_____

_____

_____

Do the students in your youth group hunger for wisdom? How
can you develop that hunger in them? _____

_____

_____

_____

_____

_____

_____

_____

_____

_____

_____

_____

_____

Checkpoint #5
Wise Choices
Walking Wisely in a Fool's World

Principle

Walk wisely.

Critical Question

Are your students making wise choices in every area of their lives?

Key Passage

Ephesians 5:15–17

May God grant us the wisdom
to discover the right,
the will to choose it,
and the strength
to make it endure.

—KING ARTHUR
in *First Knight*

Wise Choices

Walking Wisely in a Fool's World

Whenever teenagers are faced with an opportunity, an invitation, or a desire, they will typically pose the question, Is there anything wrong with this? Their assumption is that if something is not wrong, then it must be right. If they have never heard a sermon against it, don't know any Bible verses condemning it, or see that other Christians are involved, their natural tendency is to conclude that it must be OK.

But the question they are really asking is this: How close can I get to sin without actually sinning?

The "How far is too far?" issue we discussed in checkpoint #3 is a case in point. Students want to know how far they can go in a physical relationship with a boyfriend or girlfriend before they are considered to be sinning. Where is that line? Many of our students want to avoid sin. At the same time they don't want to miss out on legitimate fun.

Teenagers have a propensity for living their lives on the line. If life were a winding mountain road, they'd take it on two wheels at ninety miles per hour instead of slowing down and distancing themselves from the edge. Why do they live like this? Their behavior stems from their insatiable curiosity —shared by many adults—about how close can they get to sin without actually sinning.

So, how close *can* they get? The Bible doesn't answer that question directly. As youth ministers, many of us have tried to meander our way through myriad biblical principles in order to form some type of foundational answer for this question and others like it. But students eventually see through our uncertainty. And if we are not careful, they exit our student ministries with no answers to some very important questions.

- ✔ Can I date a non-Christian?
- ✔ How far is too far?
- ✔ What type of music can I listen to?
- ✔ Can I attend parties?
- ✔ Is it all right for me to have a beer?
- ✔ Which movies are OK for me to see?

Life on the Line

This unresolved tension leads many of our students to live dangerously close to sin. Consequently they fall to the same temptations over and over until they are tempted to believe that the Christian life just doesn't work.

The solution to this dilemma is *not* recommitment or rededication. As long as students are living on that line, any attempt to increase their commitment level will be futile. A teenager making a recommitment while living right on the edge of "too far" is like an alcoholic standing at a bar and swearing he or she will never drink again.

Instead of evaluating opportunities, invitations, and desires by the standard of "Is anything wrong with this?" students need to ask a new question—a question that takes them to the heart of the issues they struggle with daily. They need to ask, "Is this the *wise* thing for me to do?" In order to help the students in my youth group make wise decisions, I developed a little rhyme that summarizes this principle in a way that's easy to remember:

> There's good and there's bad...
> But that is not our cue.
> But rather...
> What is the wise thing to do?

Be Careful!

The apostle Paul encouraged the believers in Ephesus to examine all of life through the lens of wisdom. He instructed them, "Be very careful, then, how you live—not as unwise but as wise, making the most of every opportunity, because the days are evil. So then do not be foolish, but understand what the will of the Lord is."[1]

Whether they realize it or not, our students live in a

dangerous world—one that is designed to destroy their minds, their bodies, their relationships, and their self-esteem. That is why Paul says "the days are evil." They were evil then, and they are evil now.

I cannot imagine being sixteen in this generation. Yet God has given us the charge of loving and protecting the teenagers in our care as they navigate their way through adolescence. We need to echo the words of Paul: "Be very careful." That term *careful* carries with it the idea of scoping out a situation. Clearly God wants our students to learn how to anticipate trouble, not walk blindly into it. He wants them to anticipate things that could be harmful before it is too late to avoid them.

No Foolishness Allowed

In dangerous environments people take extraordinary precautions. Think of all the equipment a fireman puts on before rushing into a burning building. Or think of all the checks, double-checks, and triple-checks NASA goes through before sending a manned shuttle into space. The environment demands such meticulous measures. That's why Paul goes on to say, "Therefore do not be foolish." In other words, students must never lose sight of the nature of what is going on around them. They cannot approach life blindly, as if all is well.

Most of us know from experience that we are just one decision away from doing irreversible damage to our lives and relationships. Time and maturity have taught us this. Many of us have scars that won't allow us to forget. But our students are naive. And in their naiveté they are prone to approach their world as if it is a safe place. Part of our responsibility is to paint a realistic picture of what is lurking out there in the "real world." Then, after warning our students, we must equip them with the tools they need to help them steer clear of those relationships and opportunities that have the potential to hurt them.

Wisdom is one of God's primary navigational tools for life. If we can teach students to run everything that comes their way through the grid of "Is this the wise thing to do?" they will have taken a big step toward preparing themselves to survive and even thrive in these evil days.

Facing the Truth

The apostle Paul followed his admonition to be careful with a fascinating charge: "Understand what the Lord's will is." This statement was puzzling to me when I first read it. How can Paul command us to *understand* something? After all, if you don't understand something, being told to understand does nothing to lift you beyond your confusion.

But what Paul meant was this: *Face up to what you know in your heart is the will of the Lord.* In teaching our students to make wise decisions, we must challenge them to face up to what they know in their hearts is true. As long as they aren't being honest with themselves, wisdom will elude them.

If a certain group of friends is getting them into trouble again and again, they have got to find the courage and humility to admit it. As we have seen already, their friendships will determine the quality and direction of their lives. If certain forms of entertainment cause them to sin, they must be honest about it. If a particular song sends their thoughts in a direction they shouldn't go, they must face it. Once our students are willing to face up to the truth that is rattling around in their hearts, the wise thing to do will become apparent in every situation.

The Un-Plan

The writer of Proverbs says, "He who trusts in himself is a fool, but he who walks in wisdom is kept safe."[2] According to this verse, God promises to protect us if we walk wisely. He promises to keep us safe. But safe from what? Think about the mistakes you made in your teenage years. What would you have been kept safe from if you had made wise choices? Guilt? Memories? A bad reputation? Impurity? Scars?

Let's face it. Most teenagers don't stay up late at night planning to get into trouble. Sin and its consequences always surprise them. Nothing, it seems, is ever intentional on their part. No doubt you have heard statements like these:

- ✔ "I don't know how it happened."
- ✔ "I didn't know he would _____."
- ✔ "I didn't know it was spiked."
- ✔ "I didn't plan to _____."
- ✔ "It was the first time."

The problem is not that most students plan to get into

trouble. The problem is that most students don't plan *not to*. I have never met a student who planned to:

✔ drift away from the Lord

✔ get pregnant

✔ become addicted to alcohol or tobacco

✔ become alienated from his or her mom and dad

✔ get arrested

✔ ruin his or her reputation

But I have met hundreds of students who never planned *not to*. Wisdom is God's tool to protect our kids from the things that have the potential to destroy their lives. To walk wisely, they must be proactive. They need to plan *not to*.

A Compass for Life

What our students need to help them stay on course through life's journey is an internal "compass." The question, Is this the wise thing to do? must become so ingrained in their hearts and minds that it becomes a natural reaction when they are presented with choices.

Past Experience

The past is one tool that can serve as a compass for the present. Wise students will learn to evaluate opportunities, invitations, and relationships based upon their past experiences. Someone once said that example and experience are the greatest schools of humanity. Past experiences are not just fodder for guilt or memories. Students who are committed to walking wisely must learn how to use the compass of past experience to guide them into the future.

I remember the time a particular ninth grader in my youth group—I'll call him Sam—walked up to me and confessed that he had a "drinking problem." I knew Sam pretty well and had serious doubts that he was teetering on the edge of alcoholism. So I asked him to explain. Here is the gist of his story.

Every Friday night after the high-school football game, Sam and his buddies liked to drop in to the local pizza place. Their habit was to make sure they snagged the booth right behind the one occupied by one of his friends' big brothers. Big brother would order a pitcher of beer, pour a couple of glasses, and pass them back to Sam and his underage friends.

Sam described to me the battle he fought every Friday night as he sat there trying not to sip the beer. "Sometimes I can make it through the whole night," he said. "But most of the time, I join in with everybody else." He swore up and down that he never got drunk. But he knew he had no business drinking.

Unfortunately for Sam, when he asked for my advice I was all too ready with an answer. "Quit going to get pizza with your friends after the football game," I told him. And as I expected, he looked at me like I was crazy.

"But what's wrong with getting pizza with my friends?" he asked.

"Nothing," I said. "But that's not really the issue. The issue is in light of your past experience—knowing that you will be tempted to drink when you go out for pizza—what is the wise thing to do?"

Sam shrugged his shoulders, said he would think about it, and walked away.

Our students must understand that their past experience dictates what is and isn't wise for *them*. The compass of past experience is going to work its way out in their lives in unique and specific ways. What is wise for one person is not always wise for another.

What's Up?

Current events are another tool—another compass—that students can use to determine what is and isn't wise for them. They need to ask, "In light of what's happening around me right now, what is the wise thing to do?" After all, everyone is more vulnerable to temptation at certain times than at others. What is wise today may not be wise tomorrow.

Students tend to be particularly vulnerable to temptation:

✔ right after an argument with their parents

✔ right after final exams

✔ during spring break

✔ right after a breakup

✔ during family conflict

✔ when they enter a new school

These times of stress or transition call for a heightened commitment to doing the wise thing. There is a direct relationship between these kinds of circumstances and a student's vulnerability.

I was reminded of this principle several summers ago when I drove a van loaded with students to summer camp. Two eleventh-grade girls sat directly behind me. They were lost in conversation, totally unaware that I could hear everything they were saying.

Eventually, their conversation turned to boys. Then boyfriends. Then how far each was willing to go with her boyfriend. (They were fairly explicit.)

I knew their conversation wasn't really any of my business. But like a good pastor I turned down the radio, pushed back in my seat, and listened in. Here's how the conversation ended—minus the unnecessary details:

First girl: "Would you let Jeremy _____?"
Long pause.
Second girl: "Well, if I just had a fight with my mom,
    I might."

I almost drove off the road. Everything in me wanted to turn around in my seat and say, "What does having a fight with your mom have to do with it?" But I didn't. And after I had thought about it for a while, I realized that I had seen this kind of twisted reasoning play itself out in other situations. Students often attempt to "get back" at their parents by doing something self-destructive. It doesn't make any sense, but that's how their minds work.

Teenagers are definitely more vulnerable at some times than at others. That is why we must teach them to ask the wise question within the context of their immediate surroundings and emotional state:

- ✔ "In light of what I have just been through, what is the wise thing to do?"
- ✔ "In light of what is going on at home, what is the wise thing to do?"
- ✔ "In light of what's happening at school or with my studies, what is the wise thing to do?"
- ✔ "In light of how I'm feeling right now, what is the wise thing to do?"

Looking Ahead

The future is also a compass for determining how to walk wisely. In many ways students are determining today how their tomorrows will look and feel. They are writing the story that they will tell their future spouse and children. They are making decisions now that will determine their level of self-esteem as adults. They are making decisions now that will determine what kinds of people will want to associate with them in the future. They are making decisions now that will determine where they work, how hard they will work, and how successful they will be.

As our students begin to develop a mental image of what their lives could and should be in the future, they must ask, "In light of my future hopes and dreams, what is the wise thing to do?" We must help them understand that wisdom is God's way of protecting their dreams. It is also the surest path toward the fulfillment of all that they hope for in the days and years ahead.

What's the Catch?

There is a catch to living a life of wisdom, however. Students who choose to walk wisely are going to look a little strange to their friends. Even some of their Christian peers won't understand why they choose to "miss out" on opportunities that appear to be fun or good (or at least not too bad). Wise students will almost always be accused of being too legalistic or hung up on rules.

When I teach students about wisdom I always address this issue. Then I have the kids repeat the following phrase out loud: "For me, that just isn't the wise thing to do."

Our students need to know that it is not their responsibility to justify their standards to their friends. Their responsibility is to do what is wise. When questioned or criticized, they can simply respond, "For me, that just isn't the wise thing to do." How can someone argue with that?

Behind Door Number One

As I mentioned in checkpoint #4, one of the most productive series I've ever developed for my students was built around the three types of people mentioned in the book of Proverbs: the wise, the fool, and the scoffer. Using a concordance, I looked up every verse in Proverbs that mentioned these three characters. Then I made a list of the terms and phrases that described each one. I also made a list of the consequences or blessings associated with their actions.

Transferring these traits to my youth group, I came up with the following portrait of a student who chooses the path of wisdom. The picture makes a compelling argument for living wisely. The wise student will:

- ✔ make good decisions[3]
- ✔ live a long life[4]
- ✔ be attractive to others[5]
- ✔ prosper[6]
- ✔ be persuasive[7]
- ✔ be prepared for the future[8]
- ✔ be sought after by those of power and influence[9]
- ✔ ultimately rise to a position of power[10]
- ✔ be kept safe from harm[11]
- ✔ be a good counselor for others[12]

Students need to understand that if they decide not to embrace wisdom as a guiding principle for their lives, they are opting for something else by default. No one ever walks away from something without walking toward something else.

If teenagers choose not to walk in wisdom, what are their options?

Option 1: The Fool

Fools are those people who know right from wrong and choose to do what is wrong. They could care less about doing what is right. Fools are not guided by a predetermined standard of behavior but follow their immediate desires. They do what they feel like doing. They go with the emotional flow. Fools generally don't have reasons to explain their behavior; they just do what they want to do regardless of the consequences.

Fools will not take instruction because they believe they already know everything. The Bible gives us a vivid word picture of how a fool receives counsel: "Like a lame man's legs that hang limp is a proverb [wisdom] in the mouth of a fool."[13] As a result, fools constantly find themselves in trouble. They're always in over their heads, and they don't know how they got there. Their end is pain, heartache, and destruction. What student would want to be a fool?

Option 2: The Scoffer

Scoffers, like fools, are those who know right from wrong and choose to do what is wrong. But scoffers go a step further. They criticize the wise.

You and I know them well. Scoffers are those students who present themselves as too cool for everyone else in the youth group. They refuse to worship. They refuse to participate in

Bible study. What's worse, they look for opportunities to make fun of the students who do these things. They are arrogant, smart-mouthed, and condescending. They consistently ridicule those students who are trying to do what's right.

Unfortunately for them, scoffers tend to make very unwise decisions over time. Their decisions often lead them into a downward spiral that culminates in tragedy and destruction. When scoffers need wisdom most, it is nowhere to be found. In their attempt to distance themselves from wise people, they distance themselves from wisdom—and that ultimately comes back to haunt them.

Every student I have ever visited in an alcohol or drug rehabilitation program, every pregnant teenager I have ever met, every young inmate I have ever spoken to in depth, has in some form or fashion admitted to making foolish decisions. And every one of them thought that they were too smart, too cool, or too careful to get burned. Such is the story of the scoffer.

Our students need to know their options. They need to know that to refuse the path of wisdom is to choose the way of the fool or the scoffer. They need to understand the benefits of walking wisely—and the consequences of choosing otherwise.

Taking the First Step

Wisdom always begins with the recognition of who God is. The writer of Proverbs says it this way: "The fear of the LORD is the beginning of wisdom, and knowledge of the Holy One is understanding."[14]

We can lead our students to embrace the way of wisdom by introducing them to God as He is: their omniscient, loving heavenly Father who by nature of His position deserves their loyalty and submission. They take the first step by saying, "You are God and I'm not. You are the teacher and I am the student. Tell me what to do and I will do it. I surrender all." When they say yes to God before they even know what it is that He requires—that's when wisdom begins to be their guide for life.

Remember, our students are always only one decision away from helping or hurting their lives. As youth pastors, let's do all we can to make sure they have the tools and the understanding they need to make wise choices. With God's help and our encouragement, they *can* learn to walk wisely in a fool's world.

Checking In
Read Ephesians 5:15–17 and Proverbs 28:26
Think about It

Why do you think Paul encourages us to be very careful about how we live? _____

_____

_____

_____

_____

_____

_____

What is his solution for living a careful life? Is this a suggestion or command? _____

_____

_____

What is the promise in Proverbs 28:26 for those who walk wisely? _____

_____

_____

_____

_____

What does a fool trust in? With that in mind, have there been times in your life when you've been guilty of being a fool?

_____

_____

_____

_____

_____

_____

_____

Think about your own life and ministry. Are you walking with the wise or are you a companion of fools? Explain.

_____

_____

_____

_____

_____

_____

Using a Bible concordance, look up every verse in Proverbs that mentions these three categories of people: the wise, the fool, and the scoffer. Make a list of the terms and phrases describing each one. Make another list of the consequences associated with their actions. _____

_____

_____

_____

_____

_____

Can you identify students in your youth ministry who fall into these three categories? How can you encourage them to walk wisely? _____

_____

_____

_____

_____

_____

Checkpoint #6
Ultimate Authority
Finding Freedom under God

Principle

Maximum freedom is found under God's authority.

Critical Question

Are your students submitting to the authorities God has placed over them?

Key Passage

Romans 13:1–2

I fight authority...
authority always wins.

—JOHN COUGAR MELLENCAMP
from his song "Authority Song"

Ultimate Authority
Finding Freedom under God

Freedom and God do not mix in the minds of most teenagers. These two entities seem as oxymoronic as saying *poor* Bill Gates or *ugly* Tyra Banks. So when Jesus says that "you will know the truth, and the truth will set you *free*,"[1] students may dismiss the simple logic or potential power of such a statement because of *who* made it. "God can't possibly be talking about freedom," they reason, "because He is all about rules and regulations." So students ignore this biblical truth and search longingly for a life with little or no authority, hoping one day to find the elusive land of freedom.

Our students' understanding of ultimate authority is an important checkpoint because so much of their lives is influenced by how they respond to authority. How they respond to God as an authority will have a direct effect on how they respond to their parents. How they respond to parental authority will have a direct effect on how they respond to the laws that govern this land and to the people that enforce those laws. How they respond to the people and institutions that enforce the laws will determine their standing and influence in society.

Even more important, our students' attitude toward authority will ultimately impact their intimacy with God. It will also impact how much authority they are entrusted with in their lives.

Marriage is ultimately an authority issue. Parenthood is ultimately an authority issue. Discipleship is ultimately an authority issue. Becoming spiritually influential in the lives of others is ultimately an authority issue.

It may be tempting for students to disregard authority and never attach significance to their attitude and response to it. But as their youth leaders, it is up to us to revisit this crucial checkpoint time and time again. As we emphasize how the authority issue influences their lives in so many arenas, they will begin to understand why it is important for them to submit to the authorities God has placed over them—and to His ultimate authority. True freedom can be found no other way.

I'm Free!

Adam and Eve were the freest people who have ever walked the face of this planet. Why? They lived in a "one-rule" world. They were given only one "Thou shalt not." God said they could do whatever they wanted to *except* eat from the tree of the knowledge of good and evil. Tend the garden. Name the animals. Multiply. Just don't touch that tree.

I love to talk to students about the world of Adam and Eve. Like most teenagers, I grew up thinking that God loved rules. I assumed that He got a kick out of saying no. But in His ideal world—a world that was just the way He wanted it—He only instituted one rule. Why? Because *God is not into rules.* God loves and values freedom.

Adam and Eve were happy in God's one-rule world until Satan came along and convinced them that they were not absolutely free. The implication of his devious line of questioning in the Book of Genesis[2] was that God was holding out on them, that there was a level of freedom they were missing out on. Ultimately, in an attempt to reach for absolute freedom, they chose the way of disobedience and rebellion to God's authority. The premise of their decision was that *rebellion* brings freedom.

Rebellion was and is the attitude and act of disobeying God's rule. Adam and Eve were convinced that freedom could be found in doing what was forbidden. What they soon realized was that they *lost* their freedom because of their rebellion. No longer would they live in the Garden. They would work hard for their food. They would experience pain in childbearing.

Interestingly enough, our society is full of rules today because of Adam and Eve's unwillingness to submit to God's authority. They broke one rule. Now we are inundated with rules.

Sound like freedom to you?

There is a significant principle behind God's command to Adam and Eve: *Maximum freedom is found under God's authority*. That seems so counterintuitive to most teenagers. How can they be under authority *and* be free? How can they follow a standard of rules yet have the freedom to choose what they want to do? Isn't that a contradiction? Can freedom and authority really coexist?

The Cost of Freedom

Most teenagers believe freedom is a world without authority. That is a lie that will actually rob them of their freedom. Let me illustrate.

Bobby's parents have set some boundaries that they expect their son to respect. Nothing unrealistic or dogmatic—just some standards to live by. Their intention is to keep Bobby out of harm's way and to protect his best interests.

One of those boundaries is that Bobby will not drink or hang around anyone who has been drinking alcohol, regardless of how good a friend that person may be. Bobby loves his parents and understands what they are trying to do. But he sees their efforts to protect him as overbearing and stifling. None of his friends' parents enforce the same rule, and he feels he is old enough to be responsible when it comes to drinking.

Bobby decides to disobey his parents' wishes one night and goes out to party with his friends. He doesn't drink much, but his friends do. On their way home, with a drunken friend at the wheel, their car swerves into the path of a family in a van. The wreck is horrific. The mother and three kids in the van are all killed instantly. Bobby's friend, the driver, dies as well.

Let's think about what Bobby's desire for freedom has granted him:

- ✔ He has lost a friend.

- ✔ He has had a part in the death of a woman and three kids.

- ✔ He has seen families devastated for years to come.

- ✔ He has broken the law by drinking while under the legal age.

- ✔ He will probably be fined.

- ✔ He may lose his driving privileges.

- ✔ He will lose the trust of his parents.

- ✔ He will lose the trust of his peers.

- ✔ He will probably lose friends.

The list could go on and on. Sound like freedom to you?

Now let's talk about you for a moment. I'm going to assume that you're married. (If you aren't, you can dream.) You absolutely love your spouse with everything that's inside you. He or she is your best friend, lover, and partner in life. There is nothing you wouldn't do for this person.

When you married your spouse, you vowed to stay married

until death. For richer or poorer. In sickness and in health. These are the "rules" you chose to play by and live under. But what if you want "freedom" and decide to cheat on your spouse? You're choosing to break the rules of marriage. Let's think about what will result from your choice of freedom over rules:

- ✔ You will lose your marriage.

- ✔ You will lose your friendship with your spouse.

- ✔ You will lose your sexual relationship with your spouse.

- ✔ You will lose your friendship with your spouse's family.

- ✔ You will lose other friends.

- ✔ You will lose your children or at least time with your children.

- ✔ You will lose money via divorce court, alimony, and child support.

- ✔ You may lose your home or at least some possessions.

And the list could go on and on. Sound like freedom to you?

The point is that God wants us to be as free as we can be. But maximum freedom is found *under authority*. Breaking the rules or having no rules at all will not bring freedom. Jesus said

that truth sets us free. God is truth, and it is under His authority that we gain true freedom.

Rebels without a Clue

If you had asked me when I was a teenager what God's
favorite word is, the answer would have been simple and
quick: "No!"

In fact it would have been my humble opinion that the
entire Bible could be reduced to that one word. (If only nar-
rowing the mammoth truths of Scripture into one concise
statement were that easy!) Like many students today, I was
convinced that God was a legalistic, outdated geezer with no
clue about "real people" and "real life." And since His answer
was always no, the only recourse was rebellion. After all, I figured, the universe revolved around me, and it was my right to
enjoy this brief journey called life.

One of the difficulties of being a teenager is making the
transition from adolescence to adulthood—from a stage of life
with few freedoms and little responsibility to a stage of life
with more freedom and greater responsibility. During these
years the tendency of most teenagers is to see their authorities
as their enemies. Parents, police, and pastors are the people
holding them back from the freedom they are certain they can
handle and feel they deserve. Many are even tempted to
believe that if they could just get away from home, their
battles with authority would end. No more rules! No more "do
this" and "do that"! In the words of William Wallace in the
movie *Braveheart:* "Freeeedooooom!"

Most teenagers long for the day when they can move out of the house and be free. Meanwhile those of us who are adults wish we could go back! Why? We've learned from experience that getting older doesn't mean having fewer authorities over us. Just the opposite.

Think about it. When you were two years old, who did you have to answer to? When you entered elementary school, who did you have to answer to? When you started middle and high school, who did you have to answer to? Now, as an adult, who do you have to answer to?

The point is simple yet profound: The older you get, the more arenas of life you enter, the more authorities you have. There is only one group for which this is not true: men and women in prison. Their only authority is the warden. But that's certainly not freedom!

The human heart has a tendency to cry, "I don't want anybody telling me what to do!" But authority is a fact of life. It isn't going away. We can either help students learn to live with it and benefit from it or continue to watch as student after student chooses to resist authority and lose whatever freedom they have.

Absolutely—Not!

There is no such thing as absolute freedom. Everybody answers to somebody. Even Jesus.

The Gospels tell us repeatedly about people being in awe of Jesus because of His authority to heal the sick, raise the dead to life, calm storms, and command demons to flee. But how did

Jesus view His own authority? His interaction with a Roman centurion in Matthew 8 gives us an interesting perspective.

> When Jesus had entered Capernaum, a centurion came to him, asking for help. "Lord," he said, "my servant lies at home paralyzed and in terrible suffering."
>
> Jesus said to him, "I will go and heal him."
>
> The centurion replied, "Lord, I do not deserve to have you come under my roof. But just say the word, and my servant will be healed. *For I myself am a man under authority* (emphasis mine), with soldiers under me. I tell this one, 'Go,' and he goes; and that one, 'Come,' and he comes. I say to my servant, 'Do this,' and he does it."
>
> When Jesus heard this, he was astonished and said to those following him, "I tell you the truth, I have not found anyone in Israel with such great faith."[3]

Apparently this Roman soldier recognized something that many of Christ's closest followers failed to grasp: *Jesus Himself was under authority.* When the centurion gave orders to men below him in rank, those men obeyed because they knew he was operating under the authority of the Roman state. He had authority because he was under authority. As he watched Jesus exercise authority over disease and demons, it occurred to him that Christ must be under some divine authority to be able to wield that kind of power.

This short encounter illustrates an important principle: *To have authority, you must be under authority.* The authority that

Jesus had to do His amazing miracles was granted to Him by God. Jesus was under His Father's authority. Consequently, He had authority.

Putting the *Who* before the *What*

If our students want to have authority, they must learn to live under authority. But that's not always easy. Every time I teach on this topic, a handful of students will object based upon the fact that their parents or other authorities are not believers and therefore are not operating under God's authority. What about the father who is in prison? What about the teacher who seems to love to belittle her students? What about the coach who can't stir up his team without shouting profanities?

Before we can attempt to address all the "what abouts," we must first lead our students to embrace the truth of God's ultimate authority. Paul, in his letter to the church in Rome, says: "Everyone must submit himself to the governing authorities, for there is no authority except that which God has established. The authorities that exist have been established by God. Consequently, he who rebels against the authority is rebelling against what God has instituted, and those who do so will bring judgment on themselves."[4]

Similarly, Peter writes, "Submit yourselves for the Lord's sake to every authority instituted among men: whether to the king, as the supreme authority, or to governors, who are sent by him to punish those who do wrong and to commend those who do right."[5]

These two scriptures are the backbone of the Ultimate Authority checkpoint. If God is ultimately behind all authority, then authority issues are ultimately spiritual issues. Students cannot pursue intimacy with God and ignore their conflicts with authority. Or to put it another way, they cannot be right with God and out of sorts with the authorities God has placed over them.

It is important for our students to understand that while not every authority is godly, God establishes every authority. Even ungodly authority. Granted, that doesn't make sense on the surface. But the Bible is full of stories that illustrate how God uses ungodly authority to accomplish His purposes. The crucifixion of Christ stands as the paramount example. God's judgment of Israel through the Babylonians is another good example.

Our students will never be able to deal successfully with unjust or ungodly authorities until they submit to God's control over *all* authority. Then the issue is not *what* they are being asked to do. The issue is *who* is doing the asking. This is what I tell the students in my youth group:

**When someone tells you what to do,
the issue is not *what* but *who*.**

Teenagers have a tendency to evaluate a rule or request based upon its merits. If they think a rule or request is reasonable—if it makes sense to them or fits in with their plans or doesn't get in their way—they comply. But if students think that a rule or request is *not* reasonable or *doesn't* make sense or *doesn't* fit in with their plans or *gets* in their way, then they tend to believe it is OK to disobey.

This explains why some students can waltz through their front doors at 2:00 A.M. when their curfew was midnight. The rule or request seemed unreasonable and didn't fit in with their plans, so they did their own thing. When their frantic mothers meet them at the threshold, they justify their behavior by attacking the rule or the rule maker. "That's a stupid rule! Mom, you are so unfair!"

Those of us who drive often use the same line of reasoning to excuse our traffic violations. "Who put that stop sign there?" "The speed limit is too slow for this road!" In those moments of frustration, it doesn't register in our brains that God established the governing authorities that determine traffic patterns and speed limits. We focus exclusively on the *what* rather than the *who*.

But as Andrew Bonar said, "It is not the importance of the thing, but the majesty of the Lawgiver, that is our standard obedience."[6] The question our students must answer is, who is going to be in control of their lives? As long as their obedience is based upon their own evaluation of the rules and requests handed down by those in authority over them, they are retaining control of their lives. And as long as they are in control, God is on the sidelines.

Not a Happy Camper

Rodney was not the kind of kid most people would immediately be drawn to. In fact, they generally tended to shy away from him. His appearance probably had something to do with it. He always wore his black trench coat and "Indiana Jones" hat, even in the heat of summer. His demeanor shouted of aloofness and a general disregard for mankind.

What really set Rodney apart from others, however, was the fact that he never seemed to smile. The few times I got close enough to Rodney to have an intelligent conversation, I walked away with the haunting realization that this young man was *not* a happy camper. His beady eyes seemed to stare a hole right through me, and the blank, expressionless look on his face always left me uneasy. It didn't help to know that he was fixated on hard-core rock music and the philosophies of Marilyn Manson.

Rodney was unreachable, I thought. No doubt we would hear about him one day on the police blotter. Rodney's sister, however, was a very committed believer who loved God passionately. She was very concerned about her brother. One night, because of his sister's love and persistence, Rodney decided to give this "church deal" a chance. God spoke to him deeply. I will never forget sitting down with Rodney afterward. With tears streaming down his face, he could barely explain what was going on inside of him. What came out was his story.

I had known that Rodney's mom and dad were divorced, but I didn't know why. It turned out that Rodney's father was in prison. Rodney had idolized his dad and put his trust in him, only to be crushed by his arrest. What poured out of Rodney that night was the anger, frustration, resentment, and distrust that had built up over a period of time. It had shaped

Rodney's personality. It had forged his moral structure. It had stolen any peace and joy he had ever had.

Because Rodney looked on his father now with anger and disgust, he gave no other authority in his life any respect or leverage. In fact, he did exactly the opposite. He rebelled against his mom. He rebelled against society. He rebelled against God. Anyone considered an authority by the world's standards was an enemy to Rodney—including me.

Rodney's story is not unlike the stories of countless teenagers we interact with every day in our ministries. Whether they are extremists like Rodney or simply normal students having trouble obeying their parents, most teenagers struggle with the issue of authority. The underlying issue for Rodney was his loss of respect and faith in his father as a godly authority in his life. The greater issue, however, was his unwillingness to recognize and submit to God's control over *all* authority.

Once Rodney began to understand and embrace this profound truth, we began to watch a wonderful transformation take place. Slowly but surely Rodney became more trusting of authority. He gradually allowed God into places that he had kept closed in his rebellion. He still wears the trench coat and hat, but Rodney's submission to God's authority has created a foundation for other authorities to have leverage in his life.

Get It Right

Let's face it: To ignore or rebel against authority is to rebel against God. Our students' attitude and response to the authorities in their lives are ultimately their attitude and response to God. They cannot be in rebellion against a God-appointed authority and be in fellowship with God. It's impossible.

If teenagers are rebelling against their parents, for example, they will have a hard time feeling close to God. I can't tell you how many times I have had students come to me burdened by their lack of intimacy with God, only to find out that there is tension and rebellion at home. Students can recommit themselves to God time and time again, but their sense of closeness to Him will be short-lived and eventually fade away until they deal with their attitude and response to their parents.

For teenagers to seek God's will about something while living in rebellion against authority is futile. We all know students who express sincere passion about their relationship with Christ but refuse to come under the authority of their parents. Oftentimes these are the same students who have difficulty discerning God's will when it comes to their choice of friends and their plans for the future.

On the other hand, we also know students whose spiritual growth suddenly shifted into overdrive when they surrendered to the authorities God had placed in their lives. Looking back they would agree that the catalyst for their growth spurt was their decision to submit to their parents and acknowledge God's ultimate authority.

To get things right with God, teenagers must get things right with Mom and Dad. That simple act of submission to authority can serve as the defining moment for change in their lives.

The Battle Nobody Wins

Those teenagers who continue to rebel against authority will find themselves engaged in a never-ending battle that they can't win. All of their scheming and efforts to find ways around the rules will eventually come back to haunt them. Authority doesn't go away. As the great "philosopher" John Cougar Mellencamp says so eloquently, "I fight authority...authority always wins."

Our students need to understand that rebellion always has consequences. God never blesses or approves of rebellion. Jonah, with his racist heart, chose to rebel against God's authority, and he spent several nights inside Moby Dick feasting on seaweed and sardines. David, with his perverted mind, chose to rebel against God's authority, and his adulterous relationship with Bathsheba evolved into an ancient-day soap opera of murder, illegitimacy, and war.

When students resist God's authority and control, they resist the control of the One who loves them most—the only One who always has their best interests in mind. That's the real tragedy.

That's Not Fair!

Even rebellion against unjust authority has consequences. Isn't it interesting that Jesus stopped Peter from defending Him against the unjust authorities that came to arrest Him in the garden? The group of priests and soldiers that arrested Jesus acted unjustly and illegally. Yet Jesus refused to rebel or encourage rebellion.

An incident that occurred during a 1999 National Football League game illustrates what can happen when an individual goes up against authority that is clearly in error. During a game between the Jacksonville Jaguars and the Cleveland Browns, referee Jeff Triplette threw his penalty flag—weighted with BBs—toward the line of scrimmage and accidentally struck Cleveland offensive lineman Orlando Brown in the eye.

Brown knelt down in pain, and the official rushed to his side to see if he was OK. Brown staggered toward the team bench then suddenly turned and stormed back in rage toward the apologetic official.

Gesturing toward his eye, the six-foot-seven, 350-pound Brown approached Triplette and flattened the official with a two-handed shove to the chest. Brown might have done more damage if he hadn't been restrained by his teammates.

Although being hit in the eye by an inadvertent penalty flag was unfortunate and unfair, Brown still needed to respect the authority of the official. Brown's violent reaction to authority netted him a fine of thousands of dollars. He also lost at least two months of his salary and was suspended indefinitely from the NFL.

Rebellion never goes without consequences.

A Better Strategy

In every youth group there is always a student who raises another issue at this point: What about unjust authorities who require those under their authority to participate in actions that are clearly immoral or illegal? What's a believer to do?

The Scriptures are filled with examples of men and women who were required by their authorities to do things that were in direct conflict with God's commands. What we find in both the Old and New Testaments are men and women who did two things. First, they addressed their authorities directly with their intentions not to obey. Second, they willingly accepted the consequences. The one notable exception is Daniel.

The story of Daniel provides students with a wonderful model. When faced with a command from the king that went against God's law and Daniel's conscience, Daniel made his intentions clear and signaled that he was willing to accept the consequences. But he also suggested an alternative to the king's edict that was agreeable to those in authority over him. He didn't rebel, and he didn't sin.

We can encourage our students to use this strategy when they are asked or pressured by an authority to do something that they find offensive. Suggesting an alternative may very well provide them with a way out. For example, what if a teacher asks them to do a report on an objectionable topic? Instead of refusing to do the work, the students can go to the teacher and suggest an alternative subject. They must understand, of course, that if the teacher does not accept the proposal, then they must accept the consequences.

Another option is to appeal to a higher authority (the principal or department head in our example). Paul modeled this strategy after his arrest in Jerusalem. On the basis of his Roman citizenship, he appealed his case to Rome and was spared a mob trial and painful flogging.[7]

The point is that our students can find ways to stand up for their convictions without resorting to rebellion. The Bible gives them many good examples. If they learn to use these approaches rather than rebel, they will come to understand what it means to find maximum freedom under God's authority.

The Critical Question

The critical question for youth leaders is this: Are our students submitting to the authorities God has placed over them? We've already shown that our teenagers' attitude toward authority will impact every facet of their lives. But the issue of authority goes beyond their relationships with the law, school, and family. There are deeper, more fundamental issues at stake. Their attitude toward authority will impact their ability to trust, submit, and influence others throughout their lives.

Can I Trust You?

Trust is an important but often missing ingredient in life. Untrustworthy people have a difficult time trusting. People who can't trust find it impossible to maintain long-term relationships.

Trust, or faith, is also the central concept of Christianity. The very soul of our relationship with God involves trust. In one sense faith is simply a proper response to God's authority. Students will only become fully devoted followers of Christ when they learn to trust God as their ultimate authority.

My coauthor's son, Grant, believes that his dad can do almost anything. To Grant, Stuart is the strongest man in the entire world. And next to Vince Carter and Grant Hill, he is the greatest basketball player ever. Anyone who tries to convince Grant otherwise is eligible for confrontation. Stuart says:

> This implicit trust is apparent every time Grant and I shoot baskets. I give him pointers, and he willingly follows my direction because he has trust in me as an authority. It is also apparent when we visit the playground and he jumps from the top of the sliding tower into my arms. His trust that I will catch him is a result of his seeing me as an authority figure in his life. He doesn't question my strength with each jump; he knows I can and will catch him. As a result he is willing to follow my leading even when it seems risky or scary.

As youth leaders, we want our students to develop that same kind of trust in their heavenly Father. He *can* do anything. They can follow Him anywhere He leads because He will always be there to catch them. Students who learn to trust God become trustworthy themselves.

Submission

To most Christians, submission is a concept that has more to do with wives and husbands than with students. However, submission is first and foremost a quality that is pleasing to God. By definition, it is simply obedience to authority. That makes submission a crucial element in the spiritual growth of our teenagers.

James says that the wisdom that comes from God is submissive.[8] He challenges us, "Submit yourselves, then, to God."[9] In the original Greek language, this imperative command calls for immediate action to root out the sinful attitude of pride.

Many of our students are interested in having victory in their walk with Christ. They want to conquer lust, jealousy, immorality, and gossip. What they struggle with is obedience. Unfortunately, we have a tendency in our youth ministries to produce events and experiences that facilitate temporary victory rather than creating environments where obedience to God is the focus and the constant standard being raised. God never intended victory to be our students' goal but rather obedience. "Victory," states Jerry Bridges, "is a by-product of obedience."[10] And what is obedience except submission to God's authority and the authorities He established?

Influence

Another element that evolves from authority is one that we tend to overlook. A proper perspective of authority ultimately earns a student influence in the lives of other students. A poor perspective does the opposite. How many students do you know who've been broken over the lost condition of a friend yet couldn't find the leverage to influence that friend because of some past sin they participated in together? In the mind of the lost friend, God can't be all that great if supposedly Christian students won't submit to Him.

Peter admonishes us, "Submit yourselves for the Lord's sake

to every authority."[11] When we do, we "silence the ignorant talk of foolish men."[12] Students who respond properly to authority counter the false charges their peers make against Christians and thus commend the gospel to their unbelieving friends.

Practice Makes Perfect

One of the best ways I've found to help students develop the proper perspective on authority is to allow those who are ready to take on roles of leadership in our ministries. Having college students work with high-school students, high-school students with middle-school students, and so on creates a dynamic of experiential learning that is invaluable.

In our church in Atlanta we strategically place high-school students in areas of ministry on Sunday mornings. Among other things, our students serve on technical support and worship teams in the children's ministry as well as lead small discipleship groups of elementary-age and middle-school kids. These are controlled environments that offer students the freedom to exercise their leadership gifts and abilities while at the same time requiring them to submit to the authorities over them. Through serving and leading, the students are placed in positions of authority *under* authority. They learn how to submit to authority as well as lead their peers as an authority.[13]

Maintaining Authority with Students

Perhaps the greatest roadblock we face in talking to students about authority is the seemingly epidemic numbers of fallen authorities in our culture today. Students tend to reason that authority figures who prove to be ungodly forfeit their position of authority. From religious leaders to athletic role models to those who hold the highest offices in our land, the imperfections of those we've held in high regard have undermined the concept of authority among our teenagers.

This is not a new phenomenon, however. Authority figures have been falling from grace for hundreds and thousands of years.

Consider Moses, whose résumé would read: "Murderer; deliverer of God's people." Or David: "Adulterer and murderer; man after God's own heart." Or Thomas Jefferson: "Adulterer and father of slave's illegitimate children; writer of the Declaration of Independence." All great men—but not exactly model citizens.

A few years ago rock star Marilyn Manson wrote, "Times have not become more violent. They have just become *more televised*."[14] The essence of his statement holds true in relation to the fall of authority figures. It's not that people in positions of authority are becoming more immoral or imperfect. It's simply that the mistakes of authority figures are more publicized. They're common knowledge today.

Unfortunately, we can't protect our students from the failings of authorities. You and I have no control over the actions of policemen in Los Angeles, fast-talking preachers in big ministries, or elected officials in the White House. What we *can* do, however, is work to maintain *our own* authority with students.

Being *under* authority as a youth leader has taught me

invaluable lessons about the power of authority and the importance of maintaining that authority with students. Much of our success in teaching this checkpoint rests in our ability to maintain that authority and respect. How do we accomplish this? I believe there are five keys:

Authenticity

Students are not expecting perfection from us. They have the rare ability—unlike adults—to not expect more of others than they can expect of themselves. What they *do* demand is authenticity. The most crippling trait for an authority figure is to be "not real." When I've seen policemen try to gain control of volatile situations with students, the authentic and transparent officer is always the one who gains the respect and response of the kids—not the one who thinks he is God's gift to the SWAT team. Authenticity is crucial.

Consistency

Where we go and what we do advertises who we are. The gods we serve paint themselves on our faces and our lives. Students see these things, and they aren't fooled.

Hypocrisy in an authority figure is deadly. It may be the one thing that teenagers hate the most. Students are quick to dismiss "do-what-I-say-not-what-I-do" leadership. They want to see consistency between our words and our actions, between what we say we believe and how we live. Then they'll listen.

Giftedness

I mention giftedness not because it is a critical trait for a youth leader, but because many youth leaders make the fatal mistake of assuming that their giftedness determines their effectiveness as an authority in their students' lives. If authenticity and consistency are our foundation, however, giftedness is optional.

It has been my observation that leaders who lack authenticity or who struggle with hypocrisy tend to lean on their giftedness as a means to their end. They want to have authority with their students, and they use creativity and imagination to get it. But students never believe the hype; they *endure* it to get to the heart of the matter. And if the heart of the matter is not pure, teenagers will be out of those youth ministries in the blink of an eye.

Relationship

How many times have you watched small-group leaders lose their passion for working with students because they leaned on their leadership position as leverage with their students rather than relationally connecting with them? Leaders who cling to and manipulate their position as leverage eventually lose their authority in the eyes of their students.

If we want our authority to be influential, it must be based on relationship. You might say that our relationship with our students serves as a "cushion" of love and trust that breaks their fall when we must exercise truth and authority in their lives.

Respect

Connected to relational authority is the concept of respect. I'm not talking primarily about students respecting us; I'm talking about us respecting our students. Teenagers today have valid opinions. Their struggles, pain, and experience far exceed anything we can imagine. They are a postmodern, electronic generation learning largely through multisensory stimulation. (By the way, a lot of students diagnosed with attention deficit disorder—a virtual epidemic these days—are really multisensory learners, in need of total learning experiences that involve more than just reading books or listening to lectures.) We need to respect our students enough to teach them in ways they can understand. We also need to respect their opinions, viewpoints, and personal expressions of individuality. When we do, they will be more willing to give us a place of real authority in their lives.

Here's the bottom line: Unless we as youth leaders learn to live consistent, authentic lives void of hypocrisy; unless we learn to use our giftedness as a tool while refusing to lean on it; and unless we learn to develop real relationships with our students that respect them for the unique and important creations that they are, our authority is doomed. Our influence will be short-lived. We will have little success in molding and shaping the spiritual leaders of tomorrow *today*.

On the other hand, teenagers will not dismiss a lifestyle characterized by respect and honor. As youth leaders, we need to make sure *we* are demonstrating a proper perspective on authority. Students will notice and evaluate our message accordingly.

Aye, Aye, Captain

The 2000 Universal Studios movie *U-571* is a white-knuckled World War II suspense drama about an American submarine crew's battle against time and their own fears while carrying out a daring mission to capture a top-secret encrypting device from a Nazi U-boat. I have to tell you, this film kept me on the edge of my seat!

Following an unexpected turn of events, the American sailors find themselves trapped in the enemy's vessel deep in hostile waters. They are at a distinct disadvantage since they are unfamiliar with the operation of the enemy sub. Ultimately the destiny of these nine ordinary men as well as the fate of their mission depends upon their camaraderie, their instinct, and their ability to suppress their fear and submit to authority.

In one of the last and most memorable scenes of the movie, Lieutenant Andrew Tyler pleads with Trigger, a young enlisted sailor, to try one last time to accomplish a seemingly impossible task. A valve that is leaking has rendered the only available torpedo chamber useless. The valve is under several feet of water, and Trigger is the only crew member small enough to get to the valve. With an air hose stuck in his mouth, he tries several times to reach the valve. The hose won't reach far enough, however, and heavy debris keeps the valve inches away from Trigger's outstretched fingers.

As the young sailor weeps from the realization that the enemy is literally seconds from destroying their submarine and he is the crew's last and only hope, Lieutenant Tyler grabs him and passionately challenges him with these words: "As your commanding officer, I am ordering you to go back and try, because it is your job!" The outcome of the story hinges on Trigger's response to that challenge, and, well...go see the movie!

If you are like me, you have wanted to have that kind of leverage with teenagers. Many students on the fringe of your youth group wander through life with no apparent guide or conscience, and your core students continually battle with the same struggles as their lost friends. You want to grab them and scream, "I know what I'm talking about! You can do this! Your life depends on it! *Try!*"

The lives of our students are movies in the making. The outcome of their stories hinge on their willingness to respond appropriately to the authorities God has placed over them. As their leaders, you and I need to live as men and women under authority. Then we must do all we can to instill an appreciation and respect for authority in the hearts and minds of our students.

They'll ultimately be appreciating and respecting God. And they find that the principle is true: *Maximum freedom is found under God's authority.*

Checking In
Read Nehemiah 1:1–2:18 and Matthew 22:15–22
Think about It

What was the relationship between Nehemiah's position in King Artaxerxes' court and God's ultimate plan for Nehemiah?

_____

_____

_____

_____

What is the principle that Jesus was getting at when He made His statement about the denarius to the Pharisees? If you were going to teach on this passage, how would you state the principle to your students? _____

_____

_____

_____

As a leader, how do you respond to authority? Do you find it difficult to stay under authority?_____

_____

_____

What is the relationship between what God may ultimately want to do _through_ you and the authorities He has placed _over_ you!_____

_____

_____

_____

What have you learned from current or past authorities?

_____

_____

_____

_____

_____

_____

What are some leadership characteristics that sometimes can be misinterpreted as rebellion by an authority? _____

_____

_____

_____

_____

_____

_____

Checkpoint #7
Others First
Considering Others before Yourself

Principle

When you make yourself nothing, you're really something.

Critical Question

Are your students putting the needs of others ahead of their own?

Key Passage

Philippians 2:3–11

The high destiny
of the individual
is to serve
rather than to rule.

—ALBERT EINSTEIN

Others First

Considering Others before Yourself

Youth leaders face a monumental task: developing students who consider others before themselves. Why is this so difficult? Read the headlines. A professional athlete has his girlfriend killed so she won't be able to deliver his baby. Two men on a sinking fishing boat fight over the only life jacket; one man stabs the other and throws him overboard. A teenage girl attending her high-school prom delivers her baby in the ladies' room and leaves the newborn in the toilet to die. The stories go on and on.

Clearly, we live in a very selfish, self-centered society. Most of us have grown so accustomed to our me-first culture that we are suspicious of any person who demonstrates a genuine others-first attitude.

Combine sinful human nature with a culture that is

constantly asking, "What's in it for me?" and it is no wonder that most of our students suffer from a life-threatening case of *me-itis*. As far as they are concerned, they are the center of the universe. Their world revolves around them. That perception is compounded, of course, by the fact that they often have too much free time, too few responsibilities, and in many cases, way too much money.

The Root of the Conflict

But self-centeredness comes with a price. It is almost impossible to have a genuine relationship with a self-absorbed individual. Our students are paying relationally for the privilege of living in their me-first world. James goes to the heart of the matter when he writes: "What causes fights and quarrels among you? Don't they come from your desires that battle within you? You want something but don't get it. You kill and covet, but you cannot have what you want. You quarrel and fight. You do not have, because you do not ask God."[1]

The root of all relational conflict is really quite simple: Somebody is not getting his or her own way. When getting my way becomes my preoccupation, I have set myself up for a future of friction. As long as I put "me" first, it is only a matter of time until I run into someone who wants to put him- or herself first. The result, according to James, is "fights and quarrels."

Like all of us, students are prone to blame their relational difficulties on circumstances or on the person they are in conflict with. But the root of their conflict is not circumstantial. The root is that they are not getting what they want.

How do youth leaders introduce this not-so-popular principle to our students? One method is to call a student up to the front and dissect his or her last blow-up with Mom or Dad. After the student finishes describing what happened, ask, "What did you want?" Then conclude with this statement: "So the real reason you got mad is that you didn't get your way."

No doubt the student will try to argue the merits of his or her position. Most students will want to leave the impression that they really wanted to do the "right" thing, while what their parents wanted was "wrong." But if you keep the interchange going long enough, it will become apparent that the real issue is that somebody was not getting his or her way.

We all want to be seen as crusaders for what is right. But the truth is, most of us crusade for what we want. Selfishness is like every other appetite; the more you feed it, the bigger and hungrier it gets. As C. S. Lewis stated, an appetite "grows by indulgence. Starving men may think much about food, but so do gluttons."[2] Self-centeredness is not a desire that is finally and completely satisfied. The more it gets, the more it wants.

A New Standard

As Christians, however, our students have been called to a different standard—one that requires them to put the interests of others ahead of their own. The apostle Paul addresses this principle in his letter to the Philippian believers:

Do nothing out of selfish ambition or vain conceit, but in humility consider others better than yourselves. Each of you should look not only to your own interests, but also to the interests of others.

Your attitude should be the same as that of Christ Jesus: Who, being in very nature God, did not consider equality with God something to be grasped, but made himself nothing, taking the very nature of a servant, being made in human likeness. And being found in appearance as a man, he humbled himself and became obedient to death—even death on a cross![3]

These challenging verses contain four overlapping commands. A careful look at each of these commands reveals both the root of the me-first orientation and some clues as to how we can help our students break free.

1. Don't allow ambition or conceit to drive your decisions.

Teenagers today live in a world that is fueled by what Paul refers to as "vain conceit." Vain conceit is the mistaken notion that we deserve special consideration because of something inherently special about us. Directing our students toward an others-first orientation involves exposing the flawed assumption that they deserve special consideration for simply being who they are.

Are all our students unique and special in the eyes of God? Certainly. Does their uniqueness entitle them to special treatment at the expense of others? No.

2. View others as more important than yourself.

Notice Paul never says that one person *is* better than another; rather, he says that we are to *treat* others as if they were better or more important than ourselves. In other words, our students are to treat their parents, friends, teachers, and youth ministers as if those people were actually in a league that demanded better-than-average treatment.

When I communicate this concept to students, I ask them to close their eyes and picture someone they have never met but whom they admire—an actor, musician, or sports hero, for example. Once everybody has someone in mind, I ask them to imagine how they would treat that person if he or she were to come to their house for dinner. What would they talk about? Would they ask questions or sit silently? If the guest asked them to do something, how would they respond? What kind of manners would they use?

You get the point. If our students were to be visited by someone they considered more important than themselves, they would treat that person differently. That's how they should treat all the people around them! Some students will argue, "But no one is better than anyone else." Remember, Paul isn't arguing that anyone is actually better or superior. Students simply must *consider* or *treat* the people around them *as if* they were better. After all, isn't that what Jesus did? (More on this later.)

3. Look out for the interests of others.

This third command is intensely practical. We must not be consumed with our own interests; instead, we must take a genuine interest in the things that interest others. Our students need to understand that their interests are not unimportant or inferior in nature. But when it comes to how they treat others, they are to make others the priority. Instead of always talking about themselves and their own needs, schedules, fears, hurts, dreams, accomplishments, and challenges, they need to learn to focus on the needs, schedules, fears, hurts, dreams, accomplishments, and challenges of the people around them.

4. Follow Christ's example of humility.

When challenged to put others first, all of us are quick to make excuses for our preoccupation with self. Most of our excuses center on the "unworthiness" of the people around us.

"If you saw how my mom treated me...."

"My dad never has time for me; why should I put him first?"

"None of my friends express much interest in how I feel; why should I care about their feelings?"

"They don't treat me with respect; why should I be polite?"

The apostle Paul must have anticipated these objections. To support his exhortations to put others first, he points us in the direction of the supreme example of selflessness: Jesus Christ. When it comes to our behavior toward others, we are to take our cues from Christ Himself. Literally, we are to have the same perspective and attitude as Christ.

To help our students understand this point, we simply need to take them on a journey through the life of Christ, focusing on how He treated the people around Him. Such a study removes all excuses. Jesus consistently treated others as if they were more important than Himself—even though they were not. He never pulled rank. He never said, "Since I am God's Son, you must treat Me as such." He played by the rules of humanity by choice, not necessity. He constantly laid aside His rights. He was a King who never demanded the deference and courtesy due to royalty.

Not only that, He was constantly serving people: washing feet, healing the sick, comforting the brokenhearted. He never allowed the rejection of others to dilute His love and concern for them. Instead, Jesus harnessed everything about Himself that set Him apart from others in order to benefit the people around Him.

Jesus willingly submitted Himself to the will of others. Think about it. The Creator subjected Himself to the creation! How far did He take His submission? How far was He willing to bend? The apostle Paul put it bluntly: "He humbled himself and became obedient to death—even death on a cross!"[4] At Calvary, Jesus put the interests of each of our students ahead of His own. His desire for a relationship with each one of them was more important to Him than getting what He deserved.

A Supernatural Attitude

Like the rest of us, our students were not born selfless beings. No teenager can do a selfless act of service and say truthfully, "Oh, it came naturally to me." We all have a bent toward *selfishness*—and that bent is rooted in sin. Because of this bent, serving others has to be an attitude that students develop. They have to be *motivated* to consider others before themselves.

But how? A servant attitude is supernatural. That's why we need to keep pointing our students to Jesus—the only supernatural human being who has ever lived. Although Jesus was equal to God, He did not consider equality with God something that He needed to hang on to. His position was not something so important to Him that He couldn't stand to lay it aside. His power was not something so precious to Him that He couldn't go without it.

What *was* precious to Jesus? *People.* Jesus considered people more important than all the power or position in the world. And He wants our students to have that same priority. We need to challenge our students with these questions:

✔ **Is your schedule of activities more important than serving others?**

✔ **Is the position you have among your peers more important than serving others?**

✔ **Is your ego or pride keeping you from stooping to serve?**

Jesus *developed* the attitude of a servant. The Bible says that Jesus "*made* himself nothing." That puts our students on a level field. A servant attitude really is possible! Jesus had to do the same thing that they have to do to serve: make themselves nothing.

Of course, students need to understand that to say that they are "nothing" doesn't mean that they are not worth anything. To the contrary, it means that their worth is not for themselves; *it is for others.* The attitude of a servant is the perspective of a heart and mind that says, "My life exists for others."

The wonderful paradox is that by living their lives as if they are nothing, students become *something* in God's eyes. Greatness in this world comes from many things—power, prestige, wealth, fame. But teenagers need to know that greatness in the kingdom of God comes only through serving others. It comes only when they humble themselves and consider the needs of others before their own.

Somebody's Got to Go First

It may seem obvious, but we need to remind our students that *only one person can go first.* Don't rush by this point too fast! When standing at the door, only one person can go through first. When ordering lunch, only one person can order first. When determining who is going to talk and who is going to listen, only one person can speak first. When two people disagree and there appears to be no compromise, only one person is going to get his or her way.

Either I go first or I allow you to. If I go first and make you wait, there is the potential for conflict. But if I let *you* go first, then there is the potential for relationship. And in God's economy, relationship—even the *potential* for relationship— takes precedence over going first. Demanding my own way will never enrich or further my relationships. On the contrary, the more "rights-oriented" I become, the greater my inability to maintain long-term relationships. Selfishness is the enemy of relationship; ultimately it destroys families, friendships, teams, and churches.

Back at the House

One of the easiest ways I've found to illustrate this principle to students is to have them evaluate their parents' relationships by asking:

- ✔ If you consider your parents' marriage to be a good one, what makes it so good?
- ✔ If you consider your parents' marriage to be a bad one, what makes it so bad?
- ✔ What could your father do differently to better his relationship with your mother?
- ✔ What could your mother do differently to better her relationship with your father?
- ✔ What is one thing your parents do that you hope to carry with you into your own marriage?

A similar exercise can focus on friendships:

- ✔ What makes a good friend a good friend?
- ✔ What makes a bad friend bad?
- ✔ What do you look for in a friend?
- ✔ Think about a friendship that started out good but went bad. What happened?

The goal of this questioning is to help students see the correlation between how they treat someone—whether or not they put that person first—and the health of their relationship with that person. This is a dynamic that will affect them for better or worse for the rest of their lives. Their answers to these questions will tend to center on issues of selfishness and selflessness. With only a little interpretive coaching from us, students will come to see that great marriages, as well as great friendships, are built upon the foundation of putting others first.

Getting Started

Let's assume that our students listen to us and accept the truth of this checkpoint: It really is best to put others first. How do they actually get started? What can they do to begin to take their eyes off of themselves and put them on the needs of others? One option is for us to send them to a Third World country for a year. That will have the short-term effect of highlighting their selfishness! If that is not an option, however, here are four words we can share with our students that represent four areas of practical application:

Listen

Students must begin to listen more and talk less. It is difficult to put others first when you are always talking. Listening communicates acceptance. Listening says, "What you have to say is important." Listening is an easy and effective way for students to put the interests of others ahead of their own.

Remember

Students need to remember what other people say to them. I know that when I have to tell somebody something twice, I feel devalued. Every teenager has had the heartbreaking experience of sharing something important with a parent only to have Mom or Dad forget about it five minutes later. (Or maybe you are the one who forgets!) That hurts.

Ask

To really communicate care and concern, students need to ask about the thing they have committed to remembering. Asking questions about what's happening in another person's life sends the message that they value what the other person considers valuable. Imagine what would happen to our students' relationships at home if they started expressing interest in their parents' world by listening, remembering, and asking:

"So, Dad, how did your presentation turn out?"

"Mom, what did Mrs. Kimball say when you told her you couldn't attend the conference?"

"Dad, did you enjoy your day off yesterday?"

"Mom, I overheard you telling Dad that you couldn't find your watch. Did it ever turn up?"

Pray

Ask your students to evaluate their prayers. Who and what do they pray about? If they are like the average Christian, their prayers revolve around their own needs rather than the needs and interests of others. Beginning to pray for others helps them redirect their hearts to the interests of others. Through intercession they tune their minds to the thoughts and burdens of those for whom they are praying.

I think this is one reason Jesus commands us to pray for our enemies. Prayer protects us from becoming too self-centered in our approach to relationships—even relationships with those we don't get along with. We need to challenge our students to pray for the people they have a tendency to be selfish around. We must encourage them to pray especially for their parents, brothers, and sisters.

The Role of Ministry

Ministry is another tool God often uses to help students get their eyes off themselves. If you have ever taken your students on a mission trip, you have seen this principle in action. Mission trips and service projects have a way of redirecting the attention and affection of even the most self-absorbed teenagers.

Serving God and others doesn't happen by chance. Students don't stumble into ministry. Teenagers never *accidentally* serve others. Serving only happens when students make a conscious choice to serve.

That is why mission trips and other service-oriented efforts are often such powerful events in their lives. Students make a conscious choice to serve God and others. They discipline their time to spend weeks or months in preparation. Often they work to earn the money to cover their costs. In that process they say no to many activities that would normally keep them distracted and instead focus their gifts and abilities on service. The trip or event itself is very impacting, but a large part of that impact is due to the investment made beforehand.

In November 1990, Stuart Hall went on a mission trip to Romania with several youth pastors. He remembers:

It was a time of many firsts for me. I spent my first Thanksgiving away from home *and* America. I was one of the first Americans ever allowed into the gymnastics training facility built for Bela Kayroli to train Romanian gymnasts. I spoke at my first funeral there— at a mountainside graveyard in the middle of a blizzard, for an eighty-nine-year-old Romanian woman I had never met.

The Romanians were celebrating a first—their one-year anniversary of the fall of Communism. They were so hungry for the Word of God! I saw one man sit down on a railroad track, begin tearing the pages out of the Bible I had given him, and hand the pages to others. These scenes will be riveted forever in my mind.

What made the trip such an impact, however, was not just what happened while I was in Romania. It was the time spent praying and preparing to go. Learning the language. Getting supplies together. Seeing God meet my financial needs, and recognizing His power and love for me. I will never be the same.

The whole process of going on the mission field revolutionized Stuart's outlook on life. Teenagers who go on mission trips have this same experience.

God has called and equipped all of us to serve one another. And He has blessed each of our teenagers with gifts and abilities that are to be focused on service. Our students are certainly not too young to be thrown into ministry or service environments. In fact, I want to encourage you to view every young man and woman under your charge as a minister—and to see that it's your responsibility to create the opportunities for them to serve! We waste our time and breath if we tell our teenagers that God has equipped each of them for ministry and then not provide opportunities for them to do just that.

Out of the Box

Too often youth leaders are guilty of limiting the concept of student ministry. But we're not just talking about teen mission trips and service projects. And we're not talking about involving only those teenagers who can speak, sing, or dance. No, if you and I are committed to moving our youth groups away from the what's-in-it-for-me mind-set, then we must look for ways to involve them in weekly or monthly ministry environments.

That means we can't get too hung up on whether or not they are "mature" enough to minister. We can't get bogged down in multi-layered training processes. We just have to get our students involved in serving. We have to push them out of their comfort zones. We must allow them to bump up against the wall of their ignorance and incompetence. We must push them past their limits. For there, in those exhausting and exasperating environments of ministry and service, God is likely to speak to them in ways He is not able to speak anywhere else.

With this in mind, the student ministry of North Point Community Church launched a program several years ago called Student Impact.[5] Student Impact is designed to integrate high-school students into the mainstream, weekly ministries of the church. As a result, dozens of high-school students serve in leadership positions that are traditionally reserved for adults. They teach Sunday school, park cars, hand out bulletins, lead worship, and collect the offering.

We've found that creating opportunities for students to minister alongside their parents and other adults goes a long way toward prying them away from their self-centered mindsets. We've also seen that students who are given the chance to use their gifts to serve the body of Christ have an easier time resisting the consumer mentality that so many teenagers bring with them to church. Teenagers involved in Student Impact show up on Sunday morning ready to give rather than simply sit back and take it all in.

Some youth ministers hear about Student Impact and think, "Great idea. But I don't have time to start something new!"

Believe me, I am very familiar with the line of thinking that goes: "I don't have time to start a new program. I don't have time to help students develop their gifts and talents. I'm too busy using mine! In fact, my day is consumed with using my teaching and administration gifts. I want to make sure the teenagers under my watch have the opportunity to participate in environments tailored to their needs and wishes. I want to make sure they are happy and want to come back next week. I don't have time to get them involved in ministry. My time is consumed *doing* ministry."

Is it any wonder that Christian teenagers are just as predisposed to self-centeredness as their secular counterparts? A student ministry that focuses exclusively on dispensing information in environments designed to attract students is contributing to the very problem this checkpoint is addressing! If our student ministries are all about *them*, then we shouldn't be surprised when they walk away thinking, *It's all about me.* To focus our attention on simply ministering *to* them is to reinforce the message that they are the epicenter of all that matters in life. But by appealing to their giftedness and their responsibilities to the body of Christ, we create a healthy alternative to the me-first world they live in.

Calendar Wars

To get students involved in ministry, however, we must surmount one more obstacle: time. I'm sure you are as amazed as I am at how busy today's teenagers are. Between homework, sports, family, friends, clubs, and hobbies, we are lucky to get an hour of their attention on Sunday! Of course, there's nothing inherently wrong with being busy. The problem for our students is that their time is eaten up by the pursuit of their own interests. This monopoly on their energies robs them of the time and freedom they need to serve God.

Few students sense any urgency when it comes to putting others first. Homework: now *that's* urgent. Soccer practice: a can't-miss! Serving the family, helping out at church, ministering to those in need: these are things that can wait…and wait…and wait. If we are going to raise up students who put others first, we must first help them develop *margin* in their lives—some uncluttered space that is available as a reserve to serve. Dr. Richard Swenson uses a mathematical formula to define this idea:[6]

$$\text{Power} - \text{Load} = \text{Margin}$$

In other words, all of our students' gifts, abilities, and energies subtracted by their schedule and time constraints equals the time they have to serve. Our students may be very gifted and talented, but if their activities and responsibilities take them to the limit of their physical and emotional resources, then they have no margin to serve. They have no time to consider the interests of others. On the other hand, if they find a way to lighten their load, they immediately create space for service. We need to encourage them to ask themselves:

✔ Is there an activity I need to stop?

✔ Is there a relationship I need to slow down?

✔ Are there things in my life that need to be less of a priority?

Change is hard, but students who want to serve God and

others must develop and maintain margin in their lives. It is the ultimate antidote to the cancer of busyness. Obviously, we are not talking about encouraging teenagers to drop out of school and set up shop at a soup kitchen. Jesus doesn't want our students to quit school. He doesn't want them to move out of their homes and hate their families. He doesn't want them to *not* have friends. In fact, in all of these arenas, our students should be serving and ministering to the people around them.

But we are talking about helping them prioritize their lives around something other than their own interests and needs. For many of our students, their busyness has diluted their sensitivity to the Spirit of God. They don't have time to listen, so they don't hear. Consequently, our creative lessons and pithy statements just bounce off. Interesting, yes. Penetrating, no.

Going beyond Words

I'm sure you desire, like I do, to raise up a generation of students who are sensitive to the needs of other people, willing to consider the interests of others first, and ready to serve. But let me ask a blunt question: What are you doing about it? Teaching won't get the job done. Simply telling your students not to be self-centered is a waste of time.

No, somewhere in your busy fall, winter, spring, and summer schedule, you must find a way to move your students out of their comfortable, teenager-centered youth-group environments and into other people's lives. Don't be content to simply minister to your students. Raise the bar. Redefine success in terms of students *in* ministry rather than students *attending* ministry. By doing so, you will have positioned yourself as a leader God can use to raise a generation of teenagers who understand what it really means to put others first.

Checking In
Read Philippians 2:3–8 and John 13:2–17
Think about It

In light of this verse in Philippians, do you think Jesus was born with the heart of a servant or was it something He developed?

_____

_____

_____

What does Paul mean when he says you must "consider" others better than yourself? _____

_____

_____

What does Philippians 2:4 say about your purpose in life?

_____

_____

_____

_____

What did Jesus mean when He said, "No servant is greater than his master"? _____

_____

_____

_____

_____

How difficult is it for you to always put others first? _____

_____

_____

_____

_____

Think of the people you will see over the course of the day. How can you symbolically "stoop" to serve them?_____

_____

_____

_____

_____

_____

Can you think of some opportunities for service or sharing about Jesus that you missed because you were "too busy" or "didn't want to get involved"? _____

_____

_____

_____

_____

Look at the mathematical definition of "margin" on page 202. How much time do you have built into your life for service beyond your ministry work? _____

_____

_____

_____

_____

_____

Conclusion

Set in Stone

Building a Rock-Solid Foundation

It is not the will to win
that is important,
but the will to prepare to win
that makes the difference.

—Vince Lombardi

Conclusion

Set in Stone

Building a Rock-Solid Foundation

Most parents spend eighteen years of hard labor planning and preparing for the day when their son or daughter graduates from high school and enters the world of higher learning or the workplace. The years leading up to that fateful day are spent investing time and money into their children with the hope that their investments will pay dividends in the future.

When students enter the youth ministry of your church, what will *you* invest in them during the coming years? When they graduate from high school, what will they carry to college or the workplace that reflects your three-to-six-year investment? Is it traceable? Is it transferable? Is it relevant? Is it life-changing? Perhaps the questions asked at the beginning of this book are timely for you today:

✔ If you could permanently imprint anything you want upon your students' minds, what would it be?

✔ What do your students *need* to know? What is the irreducible minimum?

✔ When everybody else is "doing it," what's going to keep them from joining in?

✔ When your students are sitting in a dorm room during their freshman year contemplating their options for the evening, what principles or truths should drift through their minds in that potentially defining moment?

The seven checkpoints answer these questions. If you are like me, you cringe when you think about all the students who have passed through your ministry without experiencing the intentional investment of the seven principles. We all feel deep regret for our past shortcomings in ministry. The greatest mistake we can make, however, is failing from this point forward to develop students of spiritual depth and substance.

Putting the Checkpoints in Context

We have purposefully resisted talking about context up to this point. The truth is, instilling these seven principles into the lives of your students will never happen by chance. You must develop and implement a strategy. To do that, however, you must take a very hard look at how you define the concept of discipleship.

The Big Question

The number one question youth leaders ask is, How do I disciple teenagers? Theologians and scholars have been asking the same perplexing question about people in general—not just teenagers—for years. In his classic book *The Cost of Discipleship*, Dietrich Bonhoeffer noted that "in the modern world it seems so difficult to walk with absolute certainty in the narrow way of ecclesiastical decision and yet remain in the wide open spaces of the universal love of Christ, of the patience, mercy, and 'philanthropy' of God for the weak and the ungodly. Yet somehow or another we must combine the two, or else we shall follow the paths of men. May God grant us joy as we strive earnestly to follow the way of discipleship."[1]

Youth ministers have tried to answer this question in a variety of ways, with our tendency being to *program* our students into godliness. The Sunday school model has been our most concerted effort. After all, most American students who are going to come to church do so on Sunday. Adults who can teach are there at that time. Without taking another day out of anyone's schedule, students can grow spiritually in a ready-made environment. We've also tried off-campus meetings between students or groups of students with an adult leader to facilitate a more informal environment.

There's nothing inherently wrong with these approaches. But the question is, How successful have we been in deepening our students in Christ through these environments? If you were to ask students how Sunday school has changed their lives, what do you think their response would be? That's a pretty depressing thought!

Mission Minded

The seven-checkpoints strategy is a systematic, intentional approach to discipleship that is driven by content and not context. In recent months we have seen numerous youth ministries across the country begin the process of investing these seven principles into the lives of their students. The greatest obstacle many have faced is that their overall mission has not upheld the need for intentional discipleship; or even worse, they've had no mission statement at all.

By mission statement we are implying that you must have a focused, succinct purpose for your ministry and a statement that articulates that purpose. There are hundreds of forms your ministry could take and just as many directions your ministry could go.

To *disciple* students means that your ministry must be focused and aligned in that direction. Have you ever ridden in a car that needs its tires aligned? The car shakes and rattles and may swerve to the left or right on its own. You can have the steering wheel pointed straight, but the car has other ideas. Why? It is not aligned. Operating by a mission statement can keep your ministry properly aligned.

Checking the Tires

Defining, or should I say, *redefining* discipleship is critical to developing a strategy that fits your church and youth ministry.

At North Point Community Church, our definition of discipleship is simple: people leading other people in a growing relationship with Jesus Christ. To make it something more than that is to destroy the innocence and adventure of spiritual discovery. To make it less than that is to devalue the magnitude of what happens when authentic community takes place. By authentic community I'm talking about the balance of transparency, intimacy, depth, and interaction that takes place when students engage each other in small groups. Sustained life-change is best facilitated through authentic community.

We all like to proclaim that discipling students is a core value of our ministries, but a better gauge is our programs—what we spend time and money on—and the environments we create to facilitate discipleship. Traditional Sunday school and youth meetings as most of us know them do not support authentic community. They *can*, but a major shift in thinking must take place:

- ✔ A priority must be placed on creating an environment where transparency and authenticity can occur.

- ✔ Adult leaders must make the shift from teacher/lecturer to mentor.

- ✔ Adult leaders must be trained in facilitating conversation as opposed to getting through a lesson plan.

- ✔ A shift must be made from the idea of dispersing information to sharing one central principle.

✔ That same shift must be made from the idea that
   students need to hear every verse in the Bible
   during their tenure in our ministries to a focus
   on understanding key passages.

Please note: I am talking about Sunday school *as most of us have known it and most students have experienced it.* Some churches have created an authentic and intimate environment for the Sunday school hour—but those churches are few and far between. And as a very wise sage once said, "If the horse is dead…dismount!"

It is not that programming is *bad.* In fact, programs are the primary method we have in youth ministry to accomplish the monumental task of growing students spiritually. Sunday school is not the enemy unless it has become a sacred cow. But is it the optimum environment for facilitating life-change?

Keys to Effectiveness

There are three keys to the effectiveness of the seven-checkpoints strategy in leading students into a growing relationship with Jesus Christ:

1. The seven-checkpoints strategy is relationally driven.

By relationally driven we mean that the success of students understanding and applying the seven checkpoints relies heavily on the investment of adult volunteers in your students' lives. Programs don't change people. *People* change people. Teaching must take place, but the core of discipleship happens in authentic community. The best context for instilling the checkpoints is in small groups of students led by trustworthy adults.

This week, call several of your students who've graduated from high school or college. Ask them what they remember most about your ministry and what made the greatest impact on their lives. I can almost guarantee that their answers will involve people, not information. Whatever principles have been built into their lives were probably riveted there because of a relationship with someone—maybe you. I recently overheard the mother of one of my former students (now a college graduate) telling another mom that her daughter keeps a statement I often made about dating in a visible place in her apartment. She is living by that principle today.

2. The seven-checkpoints strategy is a process.

It is fragile thinking to assume that we can deem a student discipled after a year, an eight-week course, or at the completion of certain requirements. Discipleship is never-ending. Again, I am afraid we have erred on the programmatic side in this regard. It is a mistake to over-program discipleship. Structure is a necessity. A strategy is a must. But evaluating discipleship by counting the number of quiet times students have had in a week, checking their journals, and making them recite verses is shaky ground for judging the depth of their walk with Christ.

Duffy Robbins, in his book *The Ministry of Nurture*, illustrates this beautifully when he says, "One rarely hears a youth minister aspire to build a youth group of kids who would fall asleep during prayer time. But when given a glimpse of Jesus' disciples during those final hours before his arrest, we see Jesus so earnestly in prayer that he sweats blood. Meanwhile, the three disciples that were probably the closest to him are sound asleep in a flowerbed, perhaps, at best, dreaming about prayer! These are real-life disciples? People will know you are my disciples by the ears you cut off each other?"[2]

3. The seven-checkpoints strategy is product minded.

The goal of discipleship must be students growing in their relationship with Jesus Christ. Too many of our discipleship programs are more about the program, the literature, or the teaching. The seven-checkpoints strategy is about the *students*.

As youth leaders, our target must be what we want students to look like ten or twenty years in the future. We have a tendency to be consumed with the *now* as it relates to teenagers. The reason is obvious. Parents want their kids to stay out of trouble, not get pregnant, never get arrested, not date this one or that one, make good grades, be responsible, and on and on. We easily get sucked into that wish list in our youth ministries and become only present-tense focused. But the true measure of our influence in our students' lives will probably not be apparent until they have graduated from college. If we are going to be product minded, we must be able to minister in the present while always thinking about the future.

How Does It Work?

Practically speaking, how does the seven-checkpoints strategy work? Each checkpoint is taught two times during the two years of middle school and four times during the four years of high school. Lesson menus are based on fifty-two weeks per year and include:

✔ Two weeks subtracted for Christmas and Thanksgiving

✔ Five weeks subtracted for flexible teaching and unknown scheduling conflicts

✔ Ten weeks devoted to two book studies per year The books of the Bible we choose to study are those that have one of the seven checkpoints as a central theme. Sometimes we choose character studies as a specific focus.[3]

Teaching the seven checkpoints can vary in style and environment. At North Point, we have Extreme, a middle-school discipleship environment, which meets on Sunday mornings from 9:00–10:15 A.M. We also have Inside Out, our high-school discipleship environment, which meets on Sunday afternoons from 4:30–6:30 P.M.

Worship is important in these environments. Our students begin by spending thirty to forty-five minutes in intense worship and praise. The goal of this time is to honor and glorify God while preparing the students' hearts and minds for the checkpoint that will be taught.

Afterward a "master teacher" teaches for no more than twenty-five minutes, sharing a central principle from a key Bible passage in a way that is memorable, understandable, and applicable to teenagers. Students then break into small groups according to gender, grade, and school for about thirty to forty-five minutes. Each group is led by a trustworthy adult who models Christ with passion and consistency. We ask each small-group leader to develop mentor relationships with their students. The leader's job is not to reteach the checkpoint but to ask questions that facilitate thought and conversation about it. He or she concludes the group time by giving the students a challenge for applying the checkpoint in the coming week.

In the high-school ministry we move small-group leaders up with their students each year until their students graduate. After graduation, the leaders take on an incoming class of freshmen.

Do you have to set up your ministry like ours? Not at all. When and where you choose to teach the seven checkpoints will depend on your specific situation. It may be that you can't disciple students anywhere but Sunday school. Perhaps you already do cell groups in homes. Or maybe you are in a position to wipe your proverbial slate clean and start from scratch. *When* and *where* are not as important as *how* you create the environment for discipleship.

Welcome Home

At North Point, we like to talk about environments in the context of someone visiting your home.

The Foyer Environment

If a total stranger knocked on your door, that person's first impression of you and your home would come in the foyer.

That is why the foyer of your home needs to be as warm, friendly, and inviting as possible. Otherwise, your conversation will never get past the formal. We compare this to our environment for students who have no clue about God, the Bible, or church. We want to make that environment as warm, friendly, and inviting to a lost person as we can without compromising the truth.

The Living Room Environment

If you invited someone to come in from the cold and sit and talk, you would most likely invite that person to join you in the living room of your home. This environment is not as formal as your foyer but not really the most transparent environment in your house, either. Conversation may take place but not at great depths of honesty or disclosure. Unfortunately, whether it is Sunday school or small groups, most youth-ministry discipleship environments tend to be more like a living room than an environment that promotes authentic community. That would explain why students don't share, talk, or sometimes even listen.

The Kitchen Table Environment

If you invited someone to sit at your kitchen table, then you must know and trust that person. The kitchen table is an intimate place. I know I experience some of the greatest moments of truth, honesty, candor, and transparency with my own children at our kitchen table. This is the type of environment that best facilitates the seven-checkpoints strategy.

If you want to talk about introductory ideas about God, the Bible, and Jesus, then by all means build a foyer environment. If you want to go one step deeper but not experience full disclosure, then build a living room environment. But if you want to encourage honesty and transparency and grow true disciples, you must create a kitchen table environment. As we have stated over and over, this environment can be created in Sunday school or at some other time or place that works for you. We do feel strongly, however, that small groups are crucial to an environment of discipleship and authentic community.

Checkpoints in the Foyer

Once you become purposeful with your discipleship environment, the likelihood of non-Christian students attending that environment will be very low. They won't be comfortable at the kitchen table. However, they may be willing to give an outreach environment—the foyer—a chance. As we stated in the introduction, at North Point we communicate one checkpoint per month in both our outreach and discipleship environments. At Inside Out (our discipleship environment) we go much more in-depth; students are challenged, and the accountability is high. At Rush Hour (our outreach environment) we take the same principles and communicate them in a seeker-friendly way. We use video, drama, and music that students identify with to communicate the checkpoint. Students are challenged, in a nonthreatening atmosphere, to think about one single principle.

Camp Checkpoint

The seven checkpoints can serve as your content, theme, and focus for events like summer camp, weekend retreats, and mission trips. By having a strategy for what you will communicate throughout the year, your special event planning can be more focused. Instead of using a cool T-shirt design as your inspiration, you can use a specific truth to guide you in mapping out each event. You end up with more time to actually minister to students. Your students, meanwhile, have the opportunity to focus on one critical area of their lives for an extended period of time.

Nice Arrangement

As we have stated, creating a relevant environment is critical to the success of any ministry context. So how do you make that environment happen? With middle-school students we think the answer is Sunday morning, and for good reason: Most middle-school students can't drive. Since midweek church activities have been diminishing across the country, it makes sense, as a general rule, to disciple middle-school students on Sunday morning when their parents come to church.

For high-school students, however, the answer is not so obvious. More times than not churches fall into one of three categories, and the best high-school discipleship environment varies with each one.

The Locked Church

In this scenario, your calendar is basically full, or locked. You have zero flexibility from a scheduling perspective. Your calendar tends to look like this:

✔ *Sunday morning:* small groups (Sunday school)

✔ *Sunday evening:* youth choir, leadership training, and maybe some type of discipleship training

✔ *Wednesday night:* outreach event

✔ *Other night of week:* not an option; students and leaders have no time

In this scenario, our recommendation (with limited knowledge of the situation) would be to use *Sunday morning* as your discipleship environment. There will be challenges. Here are a few of the pros and cons:

Pros

✔ Lots of students will be present.
✔ Your leadership base will be large.
✔ It is convenient.

Cons

✔ You will have to work extremely hard to create an intimate and authentic environment, especially in a more traditional, "coat-and-tie" church.

✔ Your adult volunteers will have to be trained extensively in creating authentic community in a rather formal setting.

✔ As hard as you try and train, you will probably always fight the dreaded "Sunday morning" mentality.

✔ Perhaps most difficult will be the wide spectrum of spiritual maturity (or immaturity) you will have in the dynamic of your small groups. Students who've been forced by their parents to attend will be mixed with students who really want to grow spiritually.

The Open Church

In this scenario, you have one or more time slots that are open or flexible, which means the potential is there for you to juggle some things to best facilitate the environment. Your church leadership may be open to change as long as you are organized and strategic. The calendar generally looks like this:

✔ *Sunday morning:* Sunday school or outreach event

✔ *Sunday evening:* Open or flexible

✔ *Wednesday night:* Outreach event or small groups

✔ *Other night of week:* Open but unlikely

Our recommendation would be using *either Sunday night or Wednesday night* as your discipleship environment, with a leaning toward Sunday night. Sunday morning would become a foyer or living room environment. There are pluses and minuses with this scenario as well. Here are a few:

Pros

✔ You escape the formality of Sunday morning. Students can dress casually. It is amazing how dress affects community among students!

✔ It is much easier to create an intimate and authentic environment.

✔ Students who come will want to be there. The spectrum of spiritual maturity will close dramatically.

✔ The quality of leaders will improve.

Cons

✔ You will have to reshape the thinking of most of your adult volunteers.

✔ The quantity of leaders may diminish.

✔ You may have to sell the concept to a broader range of leaders.

The Dream Church

What we all wouldn't do for this situation! If you are in a Dream Church, you basically have an open slate. No program is so sacred that it can't be sacrificed for the sake of effectiveness and purpose. The only problem is that you generally have more accountability and less room for error than in a Locked Church or Open Church.

Our recommendation would be:

✔ *Sunday morning:* A foyer or living room environment

✔ *Sunday evening:* A kitchen table environment

✔ *Wednesday night:* A foyer or living room environment

Of course, every ministry is different. So many things play into what determines the best day, time, and context for your environments. We have found, however, that a focused time for each purpose is essential.

The Measuring Stick

How do you measure and track success in discipleship? By how many kids show up? By how many are having regular quiet times and keeping journals? By how many share their faith in a week? This is a valid and critical question. In fact, your job may depend on it.

The answer is simple, although not easy. Most youth leaders have been trained and now operate in environments where statistics and numbers are the gauge for measuring success and failure. "How many" may be the operative phrase in your world.

But at North Point, we think discipleship is best measured by *stories*. Since we are talking about the process of a growing relationship with Christ, we think spiritual growth is best marked by the personal stories we hear from lives that are being transformed by truth. Let's be honest. When your ministry is based on programs, then statistics are the obvious source of measurement. However, when the focus of your ministry is people connecting in authentic community, the stories of life-change become the victories and marks of progress.

The following is a letter written to one of our small-group leaders by one of the girls in her group last year. Listen to her story:

I was watching the TV show *Felicity* Sunday after church. If you haven't seen it before it is about this girl in college who runs into all kinds of living problems. In this particular episode she was learning to cope with change. As she was ending the show she said something that reminded me of my own situation. She said, "The hardest thing about moving forward is not looking back." I think what really struck me about this is that I do look back. I look back and remember all of the awful things I've done. How could anyone ever forgive me for those things? I can't even forgive myself! On top of that

I don't know how to forgive myself until the people I have hurt the most can forgive me.

Before I got caught for all the terrible things I had been doing, I remember wanting to change. I used to remind myself at least twice a day how much I hated myself. You know what? You are right. God is working on me, and he is using my mom to do it. Now I am pretty sure she does not know that, but I do. You see, what happened is she found something in my purse that pretty much gave away exactly what I was doing and where I was headed. You know what she said to me? She said, "Most parents would have probably wished they had never opened up your purse to find those pills, but I am glad I did."

At first I was not sorry for what I had done, but I was sorry for the fact that I had gotten caught. Then I really thought about it. I know God knew I wanted to change because I told him. I obviously needed help though. I believe God asked my mom to find out to help save me. You know what else I believe? That God loves me. He must. He has not only blessed me with my mom, who is definitely making a huge impact in how and who I am changing into. He has blessed me with North Point, caring friends from work, supportive friends from school, you (what you have already done for me and will do for me I will never be able to thank you enough) and many others.

I can't remember when this was, but one week at Rush Hour we were talking about how God has a purpose for everyone. What do you think my purpose is? Am I supposed to figure that out myself, or will He kind of show me what it is? Maybe my purpose here is to share God's love with others like you do and did when you were my age. I hope so. I have already tried to make it my purpose. It is happening slowly, but it is happening. So you don't have to worry about me turning back, because I won't. I guess the conclusion to this journal entry (or whatever I have been writing) is I am ready. To give my life to God. I will need some assistance.

Since I have told you, the only person left to tell is Him. So I am going to end this entry. I have some big news to tell Someone that I'm pretty sure He has been waiting a long time to hear.

Can there be any better measure of success?

Checking In
Read All Four Gospels
Think about It

Did Jesus communicate differently in different environments?

_____

_____

_____

Record an example of a foyer environment, a living room environment, and a kitchen table environment from the Gospels. __

_____

_____

_____

Which type of church or ministry do you have—a Locked, Open, or Dream church?_____

_____

_____

_____

What are the determining factors that make your ministry situation what it is?_____

_____

_____

_____

_____

_____

Are your adult leaders operating as teachers or mentors? Why?

_____

_____

_____

_____

_____

Do your students sense authentic community and interact transparently in your present discipleship environment? Why or why not? _____

_____

_____

_____

_____

_____

Can your mission statement support the seven-checkpoints strategy? Why or why not? _____

_____

_____

_____

_____

_____

_____

What changes need to be made in your church or ministry to implement the seven-checkpoints strategy? _____

_____

_____

_____

_____

_____

Appendix 1

Lesson Menus for Middle and High School

Two-Year Middle-School Lesson Menu

Year One

Weeks	Checkpoint	Bottom Line
1–5	Authentic Faith	What is faith?
6–10	Spiritual Disciplines	Personal time with God
11–15	Moral Boundaries	Dating
16–20	Book Study	Romans
21–25	Healthy Friendships	Choosing friends
26–30	Wise Choices	Walking wisely
31–35	Ultimate Authority	God's authority
36–40	Book Study	Philippians
41–45	Others First	Selflessness

Year Two

Weeks	Checkpoint	Bottom Line
1–5	Authentic Faith	Grace
6–10	Spiritual Disciplines	Authority of Scripture
11–15	Moral Boundaries	Thought life
16–20	Book Study	James
21–25	Healthy Friendships	Accountability
26–30	Wise Choices	Will of God
31–35	Ultimate Authority	Servant leadership
36–40	Book Study	Ephesians
41–45	Others First	Submission

Four-Year High-School Lesson Menu

Year One

Weeks	Checkpoint	Bottom Line
1–5	Authentic Faith	Salvation
6–10	Spiritual Disciplines	Personal time with God
11–15	Moral Boundaries	Dating
16–20	Book Study	Romans
21–25	Healthy Friendships	Influencing unbelievers
26–30	Wise Choices	Decision making

31–35	Ultimate Authority	Parental authority
36–40	Book Study	Philippians
41–45	Others First	Spiritual gifts

Year Two

Weeks	Checkpoint	Bottom Line
1–5	Authentic Faith	Grace
6–10	Spiritual Disciplines	Authority of Scripture
11–15	Moral Boundaries	Thought life
16–20	Book Study	James
21–25	Healthy Friendships	Accountability
26–30	Wise Choices	Will of God
31–35	Ultimate Authority	Submission
36–40	Book Study	Proverbs
41–45	Others First	Servant leadership

Year Three

Weeks	Checkpoint	Bottom Line
1–5	Authentic Faith	Trusting God
6–10	Spiritual Disciplines	Prayer
11–15	Moral Boundaries	Sexual purity
16–20	Book Study	Philippians

21–25	Healthy Friendships	Peer pressure
26–30	Wise Choices	Building character
31–35	Ultimate Authority	Respecting leadership
36–40	Book Study	Psalms
41–45	Others First	Student impact

Year Four

Weeks	Checkpoint	Bottom Line
1–5	Authentic Faith	Forgiveness
6–10	Spiritual Disciplines	Intimacy with God
11–15	Moral Boundaries	Sowing and reaping
16–20	Book Study	Hebrews
21–25	Healthy Friendships	Becoming a true friend
26–30	Wise Choices	Walking wisely
31–35	Ultimate Authority	Obedience
36–40	Book Study	Ephesians
41–45	Others First	Others-minded

Suggested Character/Book Studies

Authentic Faith

Abraham

Moses

Spiritual Disciplines

Psalms

Jesus

Moral Boundaries

David

Samson

Healthy Friendships

David and Jonathan

Paul and Timothy

Wise Choices

Solomon

Nehemiah

Ultimate Authority

Joseph

Joshua

Others First

Jesus

Appendix 2
Sample Lesson Plans

The following lesson plans are samples of the material we've developed at North Point Community Church. To obtain the full series of lesson plans, turn to the ordering information on page 252.

Sample #1

- ✔ Checkpoint #2: Spiritual Discipline

- ✔ Bottom Line: Quiet Time

- ✔ Session One: Hide and Seek

- ✔ Key Passage: Mark 1:35–37

Principle

Solitude paves the way to quiet time alone with God.

Introduction

How do you create a new perspective on one of the most reviewed principles of spiritual growth in Christianity? What students need to see is that most Christians struggle with a lack of *discipline* to have an intimate time with God because of their lack of *intimate time* with God.

God's pursuit of us is based on His desire to be in intimate relationship with us. Like any relationship, you must spend time with Him for the relationship to be intimate. And just as with other relationships, the environment in which you spend that time together will determine much of the quality and excellence of that time.

Outline

I. Intimacy can be defined as being fully known by someone and fully knowing that someone without fear of rejection.

  A. Intimacy is the goal of spending time with God.

  B. God desires a personal, intimate, face-to-face relationship with you.

  C. It is possible to be good church people doing good church things for good church reasons and miss this thing that God greatly desires of us.

  D. The vibrancy of a Spirit-filled life rests in your choice to spend time with a living, all-powerful God that created you for Himself.

II. Today we are exploring one essential element of this elusive time with God: *solitude*.

A. Henri Nouwen says, "Solitude is the furnace of transformation."[1]

B. Think about these names:

1. Abraham
2. Moses
3. Joshua
4. Jonah
5. David
6. John the Baptist
7. Paul
8. Jesus

C. All of these men have a common thread in their history: God allowed them to go through an extended time of solitude before they began to influence the world.

D. We often look at their solitude as a time of punishment.

1. God looked at their solitude as the environment for transformation in their lives.
2. God still looks at solitude in the same way.

III. We mentioned in the introduction that time with God seems to be *elusive*.

A. Time with God is elusive because it hinges on a fleeting component of life: *time*.

B. Solitude is crucial because *in it you capture time*.

C. Solitude pushes out distraction and interruption. Life seems to go in slow motion.

D. The greatest hindrance to meeting with God is distraction.

    1. Solitude creates as much of a "distraction-less" environment as possible.

    2. Distraction serves as the enemy of intimacy, our ultimate goal with God.

E. Jesus considered solitude important in His time with God.

F. Jesus exemplified components of solitude that we must understand and embrace.

IV. Solitude captures time.

A. Verse 35 starts with ten words that most of us detest: "Very early in the morning while it was still dark…"

B. Early morning can be the best time to spend time with God.

    1. It is a practical way of applying "seek first his kingdom and his righteousness."[2]

    2. Jesus modeled it.

C. The principle is what is important: Time is the crucial element in solitude.

D. Whenever you can capture time through solitude, then that is a chance for you to spend intimate time with God.

V. Solitude hinges on environment.

A. Jesus did something that is crucial to solitude: He "left the house and went off to a solitary place."

B. Jesus had a place to go to gain solitude.

1. The Savior of the world needed a quiet place to go.
2. With His schedule, He probably scouted out the best "hiding place."

C. All of us have played hide and seek before.

1. Think about those hiding places where no one could find you.
2. Remember hearing your own heartbeat while you waited for someone to find you?
3. Remember that you could hear yourself breathing?
4. Remember that you didn't dare move for fear of being found?

D. Your environment of solitude created all of that.

E. You didn't want to be found...neither did Jesus.

VI. Solitude must be purposeful.

A. Why did Jesus get up early in the morning while it was still dark, leave His house, and go off to a solitary place?

1. Verse 35 concludes with these three words: "*where he prayed.*"
2. Solitude will always seem like a waste of time if there is no purpose in it.

B. Solitude *with* purpose breeds discipline and intimacy.

C. Solitude *without* purpose will breed inconsistency and apathy.

D. Jesus captured time for one reason: *to pursue intimacy with His Father.*

Illustration

I was really convicted when thinking about this idea of capturing time through solitude in order to spend time with God. Think about the trouble you used to go through—and students go through—to be alone with a "significant other." Do you remember how careful you were to arrange your time so that you could meet that person on time? Do you remember all of the effort you went through to make sure the two of you were in a solitary place? Why did you go through all that trouble?

To experience intimacy.

May we never slide into a place of complacency when it comes to seeking that kind of solitude for intimacy with God.

Small-Group Questions

1. Would you say that you experience intimacy with God? Why or why not?

2. Do you practice a consistent time alone with God? Why or why not?

3. *When* do you spend time with God? Why?

4. *Where* do you spend time with God? Why?

5. *What do you do* in your time alone with God? Why?

6. Read Mark 1:35–37. Do you struggle with getting distracted in your time alone with God? Why or why not?

7. How did God use solitude in the lives of each of the men listed below? What was their solitude?

- ✔ Abraham

- ✔ Moses

- ✔ Joshua

- ✔ Jonah

- ✔ David

- ✔ John the Baptist

- ✔ Jesus

Sample #2

- ✔ Checkpoint #6: Ultimate Authority

- ✔ Bottom Line: Who's in Charge?

- ✔ Session One: A Fact of Life

- ✔ Key Passage: Romans 13:1–2

Principle

When someone tells you what to do, the issue is not *what* but *who*.

Optional Starter

1. Have students make a list of all the authorities in their lives.

2. Ask them to choose the authority that is the most diffi-cult for them to submit to and put a #1 beside it. Next, have them choose the authority that is the second most

difficult to submit to and put a #2 beside it. Have them continue this process until every authority on their list has a number beside it.

3. Ask, "Why is it so hard to submit to the authority you listed as the most difficult to obey?"

   ✔ Is it because they ask you to do things that are wrong?

   ✔ Is it because they ask you to do things that are beyond your abilities?

   ✔ Are their requests unreasonable?

   ✔ Is the problem that you just don't like being told what to do?

4. Most of us believe a big lie when it comes to our clashes with authority. We mistakenly think that the issue is right and wrong. When our authorities ask us to do something we don't want to do, we argue as if what they are asking us to do is wrong. Somewhere along the way we get the notion that we are the ones who want what is right! The truth is, what we really want is our way.

5. It is a mature student who can distinguish the difference between arguing for what is *right* versus arguing for his or her *way*.

Introduction

One of the difficulties about being a student is that you are moving from a stage in life where you had few freedoms and little responsibility to a stage where you have more freedom and greater responsibility. You are becoming an adult. During these years, the tendency is to see your authorities as the enemy—the people that are holding you back from the freedom you think you deserve and are certain you can handle. Maybe you are tempted to believe that if you could just get away from home, your battle with authority would end.

Outline

I. It isn't going to get better.
  A. If you are like most teenagers, you long for the day when you can move out of your house and be free.
  B. The truth is the older you get, the more authorities you have.
    1. When you were three, who did you have to answer to?
    2. When you entered elementary school, who did you have to answer to?
    3. When you entered middle school, the number increased again.
    4. When you leave home, the list of authorities in your life will continue to grow.
  C. There is a group that has only one authority to answer to: men and women in prison.

D. Authority is a fact of life. It is not going away.

    1. You can learn to live with it and benefit from it or you can resist it and lose the freedom that you have.

    2. There is no such thing as ultimate freedom.

    3. Everybody answers to somebody.

II. There is one basic thing you need to know about authority: *God ultimately establishes every authority.*

    A. Not every authority is godly, but God establishes every authority.

        1. We are going to talk about ungodly authorities later.

        2. We are going to talk about what to do when asked to do something wrong.

        3. You will never be able to deal successfully with unjust authorities until you submit to God's control over all authority.

    B. To rebel against an authority is to rebel against God.

        1. Your attitude and response to your authorities is ultimately your attitude and response to God.

        2. You cannot be in rebellion against a God-appointed authority and be in fellowship with God.

    C. Rebellion always has consequences.

        1. Even rebellion against unfair or unjust authority figures has consequences.

        2. God never approves of or blesses rebellion.

III. The real issue is *who* is asking us to do something, not *what* we are being asked to do.

   A. We tend to evaluate rules and requests based on the merit of the rule or request.

     1. If we think the rule or request is reasonable; if it makes sense to us; if it fits in with our plans; and if it doesn't get in our way…*then we obey!*

     2. But if we don't think the rule or request is reasonable; if it doesn't make sense to us; if it doesn't fit in with our plans; or if it does get in our way…then we feel it is OK to disobey!

   B. When we are caught, we justify our behavior by attacking the authority or the rule maker.

   C. If God puts all the authorities in your life, then the issue is not *what* you are being asked to do but *who* is doing the asking.

IV. The First Principle of Authority is: When someone tells you what to do, the issue is not *what* but *who*.

   A. What this really boils down to is who is going to be in control of your life.

     1. As long as your obedience is based on rules and requests, you are retaining control.

     2. As long as you are in control, God is not!

   B. Ultimately, you cannot win the battle against authority.

     1. Ultimately, you are battling against God—and no one has ever won that struggle!

2. The real tragedy is that resisting God's control is to resist control of the One who loves you more than anyone else—the One who has your best interests in mind.

Small-Group Questions

1. Read Romans 13:1–2. What does Paul say our response to authority must be?
2. What does Paul say is the consequence of failing to respond to God's authority properly?
3. Do you struggle with authority figures in your life? Why or why not?
4. Do you tend to evaluate rules and requests based on how good the rule or request is from your perspective? Why?
5. What do you think is the danger in evaluating rules?
6. Do you justify wrong behavior by blaming the authority figure or rule maker?
7. Discuss this statement: If God puts all the authorities in your life, then the issue is not *what* you are being asked to do but *who* is doing the asking.

Notes

What's It All About?

1. The number of weeks allotted to each checkpoint varies based upon grade level and the topic itself. See the appendixes for an overview of our teaching schedule.

Checkpoint #1

1. Hebrews 4:14.
2. Hebrews 11:1.
3. See Matthew 7:11.
4. Hebrews 4:14–16.
5. John 14:6.
6. Proverbs 3:5–6.
7. Thomas Merton, *No Man Is an Island* (New York: Harcourt, Brace and Co., 1955), 241.

Checkpoint #2

1. Romans 12:2.
2. See Mark 1:35–37.
3. Matthew 6:33.
4. Hebrews 4:12.

5. Romans 1:29–31.
6. Mark 7:20–23.
7. 2 Corinthians 10:3–5.
8. Psalm 119:9–11.
9. Henri Nouwen, *The Way of the Heart* (San Francisco: Harper Collins, 1981), 25.

Checkpoint #3

1. 1 Corinthians 6:18.
2. Genesis 2:21–24.
3. 1 Corinthians 6:15–16.
4. 1 Thessalonians 4:3–8.
5. Ephesians 5:15.
6. Proverbs 28:26.

Checkpoint #4

1. Paulson, Steven K., "Columbine Journals Showed Anger," Associated Press, 15 May 1999.

Checkpoint #5

1. Ephesians 5:15–17.
2. Proverbs 28:26.
3. Proverbs 1:1–5; 8:14.
4. Proverbs 9:11.
5. Proverbs 11:30.
6. Proverbs 14:24.
7. Proverbs 16:23.
8. Proverbs 21:20.
9. Proverbs 14:35.
10. Proverbs 17:2.
11. Proverbs 28:26.
12. Proverbs 27:9.
13. Proverbs 26:7.
14. Proverbs 9:10.

Checkpoint #6

1. John 8:32.
2. Genesis 3:1–5.
3. Matthew 8:5–10.

Ready to invest the Seven Checkpoints in your students?

Become an exclusive member of The Seven Checkpoints Partnership and receive...

- Consultation on discipleship and student leadership strategy and environments

- Overall Seven Checkpoints strategy and structure

- Weekly Seven Checkpoints Leader's Guide

- Weekly reproducible Seven Checkpoints Lesson Guide for small group leaders

- Confidential pass code into the exclusive Seven Checkpoints area of www.dashstudentleadership.com

- Consultation support for implementation of Seven Checkpoints

www.dashstudentleadership.com

e-mail us at partners@dashstudentleadership.com

or call
678.513.7650

and ask for an Information Pack Today!

4. Romans 13:1–2.

5. 1 Peter 2:13–15.

6. Andrew Bonar, *A Commentary on Leviticus* (1846; reprint edition, Edinburgh: The Banner of Truth Trust, 1972), 218.

7. See Acts 22:25–29.

8. James 3:17.

9. James 4:7.

10. Jerry Bridges, *The Pursuit of Holiness* (Colorado Springs: Navpress, 1978), 17.

11. 1 Peter 2:13.

12. 1 Peter 2:15.

13. For more information on effectively teaching the Authority Checkpoint in a church setting, log on to www.dashstudentleadership.com.

14. Marilyn Manson, "Columbine: Whose Fault Is It?" *Rolling Stone*, 24 June 1999, 24

Checkpoint #7

1. James 4:1–2.

2. C. S. Lewis, *Mere Christianity* (New York: MacMillan Publishing Company, 1952), paperback edition, 90.

3. Philippians 2:3–8.

4. Philippians 2:8.

5. For more information about Student Impact, go to NorthPoint.org and click on the "students" button.

6. Dr. Richard Swenson, M.D., *Margin: Restoring Emotional, Physical, Financial, and Time Reserves to Overloaded Lives* (Colorado Springs: Navpress, 1992), 91–102.

Conclusion

1. Dietrich Bonhoeffer, *The Cost of Discipleship*, revised edition (New York: Macmillan Publishing, 1958), 41.

2. Duffy Robbins, *The Ministry of Nurture* (Grand Rapids: Zondervan, 1990), 54–55.

3. The Two-Year Middle-School Lesson Menu and Four-Year High-School Lesson Menu can be found in Appendix 1.

Appendix 2

1. Nouwen, *The Way of the Heart*, 25.

2. Matthew 6:33.